The Rewards of Making Energy-Efficient Choices

Experience the Benefits of Being Green

This book was created to guide you in making practical, energy-efficient choices in your home that are affordable and helpful to the environment, while also providing you with financial rewards for your energy-related investments.

David Nelmes

http://www.energyefficientchoices.com

iUniverse, Inc.
New York Bloomington

The Rewards of Making Energy-Efficient Choices
Experience the Benefits of Being Green

iUniverse books may be ordered through booksellers or by contacting:

iUniverse
1663 Liberty Drive
Bloomington, IN 47403
www.iuniverse.com
1-800-Authors (1-800-288-4677)

Because of the dynamic nature of the Internet, any Web addresses or links contained in this book may have changed since publication and may no longer be valid. The views expressed in this work are solely those of the author and do not necessarily reflect the views of the publisher, and the publisher hereby disclaims any responsibility for them.

ISBN: 978-1-4401-2434-1 (pbk)
ISBN: 978-1-4401-2433-4 (cloth)
ISBN: 978-1-4401-2435-8 (ebk)

Library of Congress Control Number: 2009927962

Printed in the United States of America

iUniverse rev. date: 5/13/09

Contents ———————————————

Acknowledgment ━━━━━━━━━━━━

I am very thankful to the writers, directors, and producers of all the informative science and technology shows on television that helped to expand my understanding of the world we live in. Their devotion to sharing innovative discoveries has inspired a new generation to think differently about how we affect our surroundings. This same generation has now begun to see how they can help to make a real difference in the world. I am a part of that new generation. I extend my most sincere thanks to all who came before me and my admiration and highest hopes to all who follow.

Preface

My work as an assistant electrical engineer on three nuclear power plants provided me with a firm belief that *quality* is an absolute necessity if you wish to build anything worthwhile. That dedication to quality became infused in every career step I followed, including many years when I focused my career on the heating and air conditioning profession.

During the past few years it became increasingly apparent that the world was undergoing less than positive change. The condition of our economy, along with our ever-growing dependency on foreign fossil fuel, necessitated that something be done to dramatically change how we create and use energy.

Meanwhile, I had become involved with an Internet-based advertising business that was doing well but did not fully answer my desire to be helpful to the world. When the opportunity arrived to sell this business, I responded quickly and then chose to turn my time and resources toward finding answers for our nation's energy needs.

Having chosen to be of help to people in our energy-troubled times, I began my journey with a singular focus that true relief could only come through the implementation of solar energy and wind turbine power in the home.

My "perfect home" would be one where electricity is used for heating, cooling, lighting, vehicles, etc., and it all comes from a renewable source that is part of the home itself.

I immediately researched many of the solar and wind-power systems available and was impressed by the variety, the complexity, and how well engineered many of these systems appeared. I truly thought I would be either selling or installing these systems in no time at all.

I live in Northeast Pennsylvania, and, after studying wind charts and solar charts, I saw a few issues begin to surface. It became apparent that if somebody in Nevada could do a job with ten solar panels, somebody in Pennsylvania would need twenty or more to produce the same amount of power.

With subsequent research I discovered that little or no financial aid was provided for many northern states by either the state governments or the utility companies. This makes it appear less and less feasible to consider the use of solar and wind as a practical renewable energy source.

As I became more familiar with the ins and outs of renewable energy systems, it became increasingly apparent that almost every good working example I saw of these systems was from a warmer or more tropical climate.

After running many solar-energy and wind-energy system sizing simulations, I found that the average person living in the middle to northern area of the United States could not afford to spend the $120,000 necessary to add a renewable energy system to their home. It just wasn't practical.

Having obtained a greater understanding of the costs associated with renewable energy systems, it became obvious why I rarely saw any in the area where I live. It became clear that I should first shift my focus to help people decrease their energy use before I even began to consider demonstrating the need to install renewable energy systems in the home.

By learning to reduce the level of wasted energy, the homeowner could gradually spend less per month on energy and could put that money aside for a future renewable energy system.

The reduction of energy use within the home would also result in reducing the size of the solar-energy or wind-turbine system needed for the home. This reduction in size, along with existing savings, could finally result in the homeowner's ability to purchase and install a renewable energy system for his or her home.

I wrote this book to share my new focus: The best way to start becoming more energy independent is for everyone to first reduce their energy use. Once we accomplish that, we can then look at the possibility of installing smaller renewable-energy systems, since the home's power demands will have been reduced.

Renewable energy in colder northern climates is affordable if you take it in steps. Make the improvements that are affordable for you today, and those changes will help you save money, so that you can afford to build what will create your energy for you in the near future.

Our media places much emphasis today on being green, and it's a good thing to want to be green, but it's not really helpful if the choices presented are not practical and, therefore, not really green. The ideas and suggestions I provide are geared toward making changes that are affordable and practical for both you and the environment.

Another wonderful result of teaching people to be more energy efficient and to use less power is that these new habits are not restricted solely to those who own homes. On average, homeowners account for two-thirds of the population, but now this helpful information is suitable for anyone in a home, whether they own it or not—and I'm much happier knowing that.

Plans are already in the works to find and develop methods to introduce renewable energy to rental homes, while maintaining affordability for both the tenant and the landlord. There are some hurdles to cross, but I believe this will be feasible within a decade.

The overall spirit of what I teach is that everyone wins when it comes to learning to be energy efficient. You win by paying less to live. You win by knowing you are creating less of an impact on the environment and our natural resources. Our planet wins by being less stressed by your existence. We all win by experiencing a higher quality of health. Construction companies that build massive wind turbines win, because they have work. Our economy wins, because unemployment drops. The list goes on. We all win.

Be energy efficient, and be a winner!

Introduction ─────────────────────────

This book was created to guide you in making practical, energy-efficient choices in your home that are affordable and helpful to the environment, while also providing you with financial rewards for your energy-related investments.

Although my focus rests primarily on the economics of saving energy and being conservative with our resources, this is not intended to overshadow the wonderful benefits our environment reaps as well.

The motivation for greener living was pushed to the forefront by the theory of global warming. There may be some debate over the truth of global warming, but a great side effect of this topic is that it has created a greater awareness that it may be a good idea to change the way we generate energy and use the earth's resources.

To better categorize how you could view any reported theories or facts about global warming, try to imagine you are driving down a secluded highway and you see a four-way intersection ahead. As you get closer, you notice you have no traffic light or stop sign, and so you have no reason to slow down. You can just keep doing what you are already doing, like consuming the world's resources as though there were no impact at all.

Now imagine that as you approach this crossroad you notice the intersecting lanes have no traffic signals either. You may have seen contradicting reports for these other lanes that indicate either massive traffic is on its way or that there is almost no traffic at all. Since one source of information is at odds with the other source, it can be confusing to select a single source to judge what to do at the intersection. This is not unlike the conflicting reports on global warming and the array of things we are advised to do as compared to those which say not to worry at all and just keep drilling.

Now imagine that you set aside the conflicting sources and simply ask yourself, "What should I do at an intersection that appears to have no traffic signals?" The answer most assuredly would be to slow down, perhaps even stop, and take a moment to look around and become aware of your surroundings.

That is all I would suggest you do with the condition of the earth's environment. Stop for a moment, and set aside all the reports that either support or denounce global warming, and ask yourself, "Is it better for the world and all people if I burn less fuel?" Ask yourself, "Is it better for the world and all people if I do my best to use the world's resources in a more considerate fashion so that those resources don't run out so quickly?"

Don't let it matter who's right about global warming, but just be happy that this issue has heightened our awareness that what we do, individually and collectively, may have an impact on the earth, so perhaps it's just a good idea to not be wasteful and to not pollute as much as we have. Perhaps it's a good idea to try to exist here without taking any more than necessary from the earth while seeking out new ways to exist that are based upon renewable technologies.

Now that we have the mindset that we want to be helpful and do less harm to the environment, it may be difficult to know where to start. Is motivation for a greener earth enough to convince anyone to stay focused for the many years of changes necessary to alter the habits and lifestyles to which we have become accustomed? Since we often tend to be self-centered to some degree, it may be difficult for many of us to remain motivated by principle alone.

I believe all people would like to be more helpful, but if we interpret change as though we are losing something, our focus and motivation may become tainted, as we revert to saying, "I like the idea of *being green*, but how will this affect me, John Smith?"

It can be difficult to convince somebody that they should change their home-heating system just so the environment will do better, but it works really well when this choice also includes their capacity to save a lot of money over time due to lower heating and cooling costs.

It does not matter what motivates you to be green, but only that the motivation is there in some form. Since most individuals are motivated by their pocketbooks, I have chosen to focus my writing on how any individual could benefit financially by being more energy efficient.

So, let's start by being practical and being open to finding solutions rather than just wallowing in the problems. To help you on your way, many of your energy-conservation and energy-efficiency questions are answered in this book. These answers are not simply based upon what are considered to be the greenest things or best things to do, but are based upon research that has uncovered the most practical things to do in any pursuit to be energy efficient and less dependent on fossil fuel.

What is a practical idea vs. an impractical idea? One such example is in reference to *energy vampires*, commonly associated with cell phone and camera chargers. Here's an excerpt from Chapter One that paints a clear picture of how to become more efficient while still remaining practical:

> Cell phone chargers and blue tooth headset chargers use virtually no power (less than 1 watt per hour) when plugged in and not in use.

> A coffee pot with LCD clock that uses a carafe and does not maintain surface heat uses 1 watt per hour when not in use.

> Overall, I found that many of the smaller things that consume minor amounts of power cost an average of $2.10 a year to operate at 12 cents per kWh (e.g., 2 watts wasted = 2 watts x 24 hrs x 365 days = 17,520 watt hrs / 1000 = 17.52 kWh per year x .12

per kWh = $2.10). With this being the case, you could unplug these items if you wish, but you don't need to purchase any special energy-saving devices for these items individually, since the amount of energy consumed to create the energy-saving device will easily exceed what your item may use over several years.

A solution for "energy vampires" would be to relocate them and place them all on one special power strip. This is often not practical, but if you could place all your charger items in one place, then, with each item wasting about $2 each year in power, you'd save enough in a year or two to validate the power consumed to both create and purchase the power strip.

As this example clearly shows, being green and being truly efficient can easily become clouded when improper information is provided. Since it can cost quite a few dollars to totally transform any home into a virtual energy-efficient paradise, the first and most vital step is to not waste money on things that really have no impact at all, even though they may sound like good ideas.

After spending months performing research on how to combine energy efficiency with affordable and practical ideas for generating your own power, I have come to the final conclusion that the optimal goal for homeowners and renters alike is to convert all or as much as possible of their home energy use to electricity.

By going all electric, with the right heating and cooling systems, the right appliances, the right vehicle, and the right attitude, you could release yourself from any dependence on foreign fossil fuels. Once your transformation to electricity has been completed, you could then choose to generate all or most of your own power if you had the capacity to install your own renewable energy systems.

When you consider the amount of energy needed to fully provide for the needs of your home, and even your vehicles, bear in mind that there is no way you could ever create your own oil, natural gas, LP gas, or coal, but you *can* generate your own electricity or choose utility power sources that use domestic fuels and renewable energy sources.

This book focuses on helping you make an "energy-liberating" change in your life—by finally freeing yourself from the bondage associated with depending upon fossil fuels and the corporations that have placed their desire for profit far, far ahead of what is best for the world, this country, and you.

Throughout this book I also provide a wide range of online resources that will further benefit you by allowing you to explore your options as deeply as possible. Simply follow the endnotes near each reference and look to the end of the chapter for that specific Web site address, then type that address into your Web browser. For example:

- One of our primary Web sites, **Greenest Choices**[1], was originally designed in late 2007. **Energy Efficient Choices**[2] was not designed until 2008.

A reference to the endnotes for all chapters, plus additional manufacturer and research information, is also found in the *Resources* chapter located toward the back of this book.

I have also provided a *Glossary of Terms* that provides easy-to-understand definitions for many terms used throughout this book.

Resources:

1 Greenest Choices: http://www.greenestchoices.com
2 Energy Efficient Choices: http://www.energyefficientchoices.com

1

Energy Efficiency and Conservation

The least expensive method to pursue when choosing to reduce energy costs is to practice *energy conservation*—that is, stop wasting the energy you are currently using. This may seem rather obvious; however, it is often overlooked, since our lifestyles often include habits by which we simply get used to wasting one thing or another, without giving it a second thought. Therefore, becoming more efficient sometimes simply consists of changing our habits and being more aware of how our actions affect our surroundings.

No matter where you live, the issues with energy use are somewhat identical. In cold northern climates, as well as in hot southern climates, our highest concern is maintaining the proper temperature in our homes, followed by concerns over providing hot water, then appliances, lighting, and, finally, general electrical usage.

To be as practical and economical as possible, we'll look at the changes you can make in your home that will provide the greatest improvement when compared to the cost associated with making the change. We'll take a look at home insulation, heating and cooling systems, lighting and appliances, drafts and structural issues, and the waste associated with entertainment and computers.

The Value of Insulating Your Home

Your household temperature should not be easily affected by the temperature outdoors. You can insulate better to prevent outdoor temperatures from easily penetrating through your walls, ceilings, and floors.

Although most of us have a general idea of the value of having a well-insulated home, it may not be as obvious how much a little insulation can help, especially if your walls and ceilings are not insulated at all.

Older Wood-Framed Homes

Most homes built within the past forty to fifty years are nearly guaranteed to have some insulation in the walls and ceilings, but when you start getting into homes built prior to the 1950s, things can change radically.

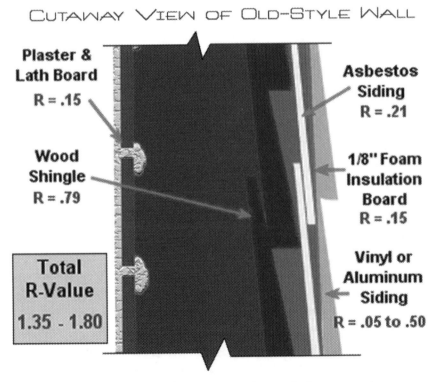

CUTAWAY VIEW OF OLD-STYLE WALL

Plaster & Lath Board
R = .15

Wood Shingle
R = .79

Total R-Value
1.35 - 1.80

Asbestos Siding
R = .21

1/8" Foam Insulation Board
R = .15

Vinyl or Aluminum Siding
R = .05 to .50

A good example is with "company homes" that were thrown up quickly to offset a housing need brought on by area industry. These homes often lacked insulation of any kind and were inherently drafty, since there was no true seal between the indoors and outdoors other than a layering of boards that served as their siding.

When looking at these older homes, we see that the outside wall construction generally consists of a layer of plaster and lath boards, a four-inch empty space, wooden shingles, tar or asbestos shingles, and perhaps an overall layer of aluminum or vinyl siding. As you can see from the diagram, even if you round the values up, the wall *R-Value* might be as low as an R-2.

What is an **R-Value**? R values are values assigned to materials with respect to how easily heat can pass though them. The easier it is for heat to pass through, the lower the *R* or *Resistance* to heat value. Likewise, the harder it is for heat to pass through, the higher the *R* or *Resistance* to heat value. Please see **_Appendix A_** for an in-depth listing of R-Values for common materials.

In newly constructed homes, the typical wall R-Value is in the order of R-20 to R-30, which is at least ten times higher than many older homes. Based upon this alone, you could see how the walls of an older home could allow up to ten times the amount of heat to escape than those of a newer home. This is why the simple act of insulating an older home can create such a major impact on heating and cooling costs. Whether you do it yourself or hire a professional, your savings could be substantial.

Insulating the walls and attics/ceilings in older homes can be performed in a few ways:

Blown-in Insulation. This involves drilling two-inch holes into each bay within each wall and using an insulation-blowing machine to force pulverized insulation into the wall cavity. This can be highly effective, but it's impossible to guarantee that the full wall cavity will be protected, since any obstruction within the wall, such as piping, wiring, plaster, and fire stops, will prevent filling the cavity as completely and as tightly as possible. Even with its drawbacks, for a three-inch to four-inch-deep outside wall, this could increase your R-Value from R-2.0 to R-13 and save up to six times the amount of heat that had easily escaped before.

Mild Renovation. This involves adding a one-inch sheet of foam board (R-5) to your existing inside walls and then covering them with new drywall. It's not as effective as filling the wall cavity and requires that electrical devices, window frames, door frames, and moldings be adjusted to work with the new wall depth, but it can be done at any time of the year by anyone with some handyman skills. Adding one-inch foam board and half-inch drywall to a three-inch to four-inch-deep outside wall would increase your R-Value from R-2.0 to R-7.5 and save almost four times the amount of heat that had easily escaped before.

True Renovation. This involves totally ripping down any old plaster wall sheathing and then properly sealing and insulating the wall space with insulation bats or foam insulation. Overall, this is the best option, since this would allow you to fill the entire wall cavity and also seal any cracks, thereby reducing outdoor cold air *infiltration* as well. If you also replace the siding, you could increase your R-Value from R-2.0 to R-20 and save up to ten times the amount of heat that had easily escaped before.

Older Brick-Constructed Homes

Another experience I have had with older homes is with brick home construction. Four-inch bricks have an R-value of .8, so even when they are doubled your R-Value is only 1.6—plus brick allows heat or cold to travel through it at a much greater rate than wood.

Not only do these older brick homes have no insulation, there isn't even any space provided to add insulation or blow it in. The inside walls may look like the same plaster walls in wood-framed homes, but they are just a quarter-inch away from the brick itself.

When faced with insulating the outside walls of an old brick home, your only recourse is to rip off the old plaster and either build an entire two-by-four wall in front of the brick so that you can install R-13 insulation and add wiring, or, if you are very limited on space, you can frame the wall with two-by-twos and fill the voids with one-and-a half-inch inch foam board (R-7.5).

Attic Spaces

In addition to insulating your walls, you need to thoroughly insulate and seal the attic space. For colder climates you want to stop your heat from rising out through the attic space, and in warmer climates you want to stop the baking heat of the sun from transferring down into your home from the attic space.

In Older Homes. Attic spaces vary greatly in old homes, whether they are single, double, or row homes, but the same principles as described for wall insulating could be applied. Many attic roofs on older homes follow the roofline and could simply be treated the same as a wall space; the only deviation may be that there are small crawlspaces around the borders of the roof where it meets the floor. These spaces could easily be insulated using either insulation bats or blown-in insulation. Since heat rises, it is very important that you don't neglect adding insulation to the attics of older homes.

In All Homes. A primary issue with insulating attic spaces is ensuring you maintain some level of outside air circulation so that condensation buildup does not occur. At no time should the insulation block airways from the eaves or be in direct contact with the inside of the roof layer.

A common problem in many attics, especially in modern homes, is that we have chosen to use them for storage. We keep our Christmas decorations up there, old toys, baby furniture, etc., and that's all fine, except that these items generally get stored on top of plywood sheathing that was laid down on top of the ceiling joists.

The very moment anything is laid down onto the joists in the attic, any blown-in insulation is crushed, and its R-value is diminished. As well, moisture can often become trapped under the plywood sheathing, regardless of insulation type, which could result in mold growing on the drywall ceiling below.

Alternatively, you can have a contractor build elevated storage spaces in the attic that do not crush the insulation nor trap condensation. This process generally results in less storage space, but it will result in your attic insulation doing the job it was designed to do.

Infiltration and Unwanted Outside Air

Although insulation can help reduce the amount of heat that transfers through your ceiling and walls, its effectiveness is greatly diminished if you have air seeping into the house around your doors, windows, receptacle openings, and cracks in the basement. This unintentional air seepage is called *infiltration,* which is more commonly referred to as *drafts.*

It's important to allow some air to move in and out of your home, so that unpleasant odors and gases don't build up within the home and also so that you have more than sufficient levels of air to breathe. Short of that, any additional air coming in or going out of the house is a waste of energy and is costing you money.

There are a few quick and painless ways to reduce any unnecessary infiltration into your home:

Caulking. After selecting a good grade of outdoor silicon caulk, you could inspect all around the perimeter of your home and seal cracks around windows, door openings, and pipe and electrical penetrations. The frames of windows on the second floor and attic should also be sealed. Whether you do it yourself or hire a professional, your savings could be substantial.

For older windows or doors that don't seal well when they close, weather stripping could be used, but this often makes the item difficult to fully close, and it is then sometimes left ajar.

To resolve badly fitting window and door seals:

- Open the door or window and place a good bead of *silicon caulk* along the unmovable wall area that the door or window normally contacts when it closes—but don't close anything yet.

- Place a wide strip of plastic wrap over the caulking, and then close the window or door, making sure the plastic wrap is more than wide enough so that no caulking comes into direct contact with the door or window.

- Wait at least four hours (twenty-four hours is best), and then open the door or window and pull off the plastic wrap. The silicon will have dried to exactly match the differences between the two surfaces, and now you have a perfect seal.

Awareness. Certain items in your home require air to be exhausted, such as bathroom exhaust vents, cooking vents, dryer vents, fireplaces, coal, oil, or gas furnaces, and water heaters. Depending upon the severity of the temperature outside, you could change a few habits to help reduce the amount of air that is being pulled into the house, only to be forced right out.

For example, on extremely cold days or on most winter nights, you should not run your clothes dryer unless it's absolutely necessary. Choosing to run the dryer during the day could make a difference of pulling in 30-degree air from outside versus pulling in 6-degree air at night. The 6-degree air will take five times the amount of energy to reheat compared to the 30-degree air.

Likewise, on hot humid days you should not run your clothes dryer in the afternoon unless absolutely necessary. Wait until later in the evening or early in the morning. Choosing to run the dryer during the night could make a difference of pulling in less humid 75-degree air from outside versus pulling in extremely humid 95-degree air during the afternoon. The very humid 95-degree air will take two to three times the amount of energy for your air conditioner to dehumidify and cool.

Even when you are not using the dryer, the vent to the outside rarely closes sufficiently to actually block the outside air, and you generally notice a temperature difference in the room where the dryer is located. To resolve issues with the dryer vent, you can try one of these options:

Install a dryer vent that really seals the vent when the dryer is not in use. This is an automatic device and requires no attention at all. Unlike basic flapper vents we see today, a good ***Dryer Vent Seal*** [1] only lets air out and never lets air in.

■ Another option, although it could create some dust and humidity issues, is to use an indoor dryer vent kit during the winter. These kits generally hold a pint or two of water that you must keep filled in order to catch any extra lint. This works fine and does help retain heat that may have otherwise been lost, but excess lint still invades the general area, and clothes may take a little longer to dry since the humidity of the immediate area can increase substantially.

If you have a fireplace and no fresh air is provided specifically for the fireplace, consider installing outdoor fresh air intakes with dampers that are located close to the firebox. This helps eliminate air being drawn in from around your doors and windows, which would result in cold air moving along your floors. Be sure to close chimney vents tightly when not in use.

Cooking vents above the stove should only be used in the winter if you have smoke issues and not just steam issues. Actually, the steam could help to humidify your home to some degree and indirectly help increase the efficiency of your heating system.

Likewise, on hot summer days, be sure to exhaust the steam from cooking so that your air conditioning system does not have to work harder than necessary.

Your fossil fuel furnace, be it oil, gas, or coal, requires fresh air to operate. The best alternative is to replace the furnace with a non-fossil fuel source—we'll discuss this later, but short of that, consider installing a fresh air intake near the furnace that operates automatically when the furnace turns on. This helps to localize the incoming air to the immediate furnace area in the basement or garage and helps to eliminate drafts throughout the rest of the house. This also prevents or lessens the amount of heated air in your home being exhausted outside.

Replace Inefficient Lighting and Appliances

If you can change a light bulb or unplug an electrical cord, you have all that is needed to easily benefit from updating your lights and most of your appliances to more energy-efficient types, even if you are not a handyman.

Reduce Lighting Costs

The easiest and quickest way to directly lower the electrical energy costs associated with general home use is to replace your standard *incandescent bulbs* with *compact fluorescent lamps* (CFLs). Not only can you save energy, but you can increase the available light for any hard-to-light areas.

For example, let's say you have two living-room table lamps where the manufacturer's guidelines indicate a maximum wattage level of 60 watts each. With both lamps turned on, the maximum amount of light you could produce with incandescent bulbs would be 120 watts—which explains the often dingy appearance of many lamp lit rooms.

By changing those two bulbs to compact fluorescent lights, you could replace each 60-watt bulb with a 20-watt compact fluorescent light (75-watt equivalent light output) and end up with a total of 150 watts of usable light, or you could replace the 60-watt bulbs with 23-watt compact fluorescent lights (100-watt equivalent light output) and end up with 200 watts of available light. You will have effectively followed the lamp manufacturer's guidelines by not exceeding the wattage levels of the lamps, while providing more light with less power. You just can't beat it.

For a clear comparison, let's measure the final cost per hour of using a 60-watt incandescent bulb versus a 13-watt compact fluorescent bulb and a 3.6-watt *LED bulb*.

The average 60-watt incandescent bulb has a life span of 1500 hours and costs about $0.75 to purchase. 60 watts x 1500 hours = 90,000

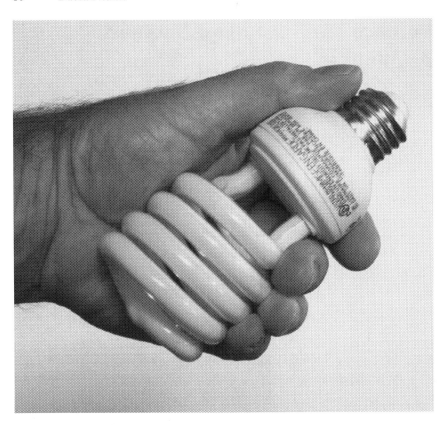

watt hours / 1000 (the number of hours in a kilowatt hour) = 90 kWh. 90 kWh x .15 per kWh = $13.50 lifetime power cost + $0.75 bulb cost = $14.25 total cost / 1500 bulb hours = $0.0095 x 1000 = $9.50 per kWh (thousand hours) of light.

The average 13-watt compact fluorescent bulb (with an equivalent 60-watt light output) has a life span of 10,000 hours and costs about $2.50. 13 watts x 10,000 hours = 130,000 watt hours / 1000 (the number of hours in a kilowatt hour) = 130 kWh. 130 kWh x .15 per kWh = $19.50 lifetime power cost + $2.50 bulb cost = $22 total cost / 10,000 bulb hours = $0.0022 x 1000 = $ 2.20 per kWh (thousand hours) of light.

The average 3.6-watt LED bulb (with an equivalent 55-watt light output) has a life span of 70,000 hours and costs about $55. That equates to 3.6 watts x 70,000 hours = 252,000 watt hours / 1000 (the number of hours in a kilowatt hour) = 252 kWh. 252 kWh x .15 per kWh = $37.80 lifetime power cost + $55 bulb cost = $92.80 total cost / 70,000 bulb hours = $0.0013 x 1000 = $ 1.30 per kWh (thousand hours) of light.

To summarize, the 60-watt incandescent bulb costs an average of $9.50 for each 1000 hours of light, while a 13-watt compact fluorescent bulb uses an average of $2.20 per 1000 hours of light, and an LED light uses an average of $1.30 for each 1000 hours of light. This means you can save from 76% to 85% on overall lighting and product costs by switching from incandescent to fluorescent or LED lights.

Data	60-Watt Incandescent Light Bulb	13-Watt Fluorescent Light Bulb	3.6-Watt LED Light Bulb
Life of Bulb	1500 hours	10000 hours	70000 hours
Number of Bulbs Used	46	7	1
Unit Cost per Bulb	$0.75	$2.50	$55
	$34.50	$17.50	
Total Cost of Bulbs	(46 bulbs at $ 0.75 each)	(7 bulbs at $ 2.5 each)	$55.00
Total KWH Used	4200 kWh	910 kWh	252 kWh
Cost per KWH	$0.15	$0.15	$0.15
Total Power Cost	$630.00	$136.50	$37.80
Total Cost of Power plus Bulbs	$664.50	$154.00	$92.80
Extra Costs vs Fluorescent:	$510.50		
Extra Costs vs LED:	$571.70	$61.20	

To see the dramatic difference between the use of incandescent and fluorescent lighting, I created a lighting chart based upon a span of 70,000 hours of bulb use. I am only going to discuss the differences between incandescent and fluorescent at this time, since the bulb costs and performance of LED lighting are still a work in progress.

At first glance, you will see where you would have to replace a CFL seven times during the 70,000 hour period, but you would need to replace the incandescent bulb forty-six times. That's forty-six trips up and down the ladder to replace those bulbs, for each fixture, during different periods of the year.

When using CFL bulbs instead, you save more than just the time if it's also necessary for you to pay somebody to change the bulbs for you. If you are getting too old to climb ladders, you have disabilities, or you simply have too many other things to do, installing CFL bulbs will decrease the amount you must pay in labor by almost seven times.

The biggest difference between CFL and incandescent bulbs is the overall costs. While incandescent bulbs would have a total cost of $664.50 during a 70,000 hour period, the CFL equivalent would have only cost $154. That's a total savings of $510.50 per bulb in each lighting fixture. In my case, I have a total of 44 bulbs when I count all rooms in my home. After 70,000 hours of use, which may take up to thirty-five years, I will have saved $22,440 in electricity costs, and that's if electricity rates never rise past the current 15 cents per kWh.

Look at Your Appliances

Washing machines, dryers, refrigerators, dishwashers, ranges, and cooktops that are ten years old or greater are using more power than necessary. I would never recommend replacing an appliance that appears to be functioning well, but as time passes and you do notice other issues with the appliance, keep in mind that when you do replace it, some of your expense will be returned to you in lower operating costs.

When choosing to replace any appliance, you should insist that your appliance be *Energy Star* rated, so that you can feel confident you will use less energy than you had used before. This rating indicates the appliance has been designed to conform to current energy-efficiency standards.

Of all the appliances you use, the biggest savings generally occurs when you replace your refrigerator-freezer, since this appliance runs continuously and receives the greatest level of use in any home. Improved compressor designs, insulation values, and vacuum seals all work together to provide a highly efficient appliance.

Next in line for high energy use in the home would be your washing machine and clothes dryer. My optimum desire for these appliances would be to shorten the length of the running time, which would reduce power use and also allow anyone to get more loads done in a shorter period of time.

Recent washing machine designs favor front-loading versions, since they use up to 50 percent less water. This immediately translates into lower water and utility bills. These machines are gentler on your clothes during the wash cycle, yet their final spin-cycle speed is much faster than top-loading washers. This faster spinning cycle leaves your clothes much drier when finished and reduces the amount of drying time, saving even more energy during the drying cycle.

Energy Vampires

A final source of power waste has been dubbed *energy vampires* or *power vampires*. These terms refer to all the electronic devices you use that remain plugged in when not in use. Having performed many tests using a ***Kill-A-Watt***[2] device, I assembled the following energy use data.

- Cell phone chargers and blue tooth headset chargers use virtually no power (less than 1 watt per hour) when plugged in and not in use.

- Small to medium TV sets, along with any associated DVD or DVR player, may use from 3 watts to 7 watts per hour when not being used.

- Larger TV sets, along with DVRs and DVD players, may use from 12 to 20 watts per hour when not in use.

- A standard set of mini Christmas lights uses 40 watts per hour.

- A coffee pot with LCD clock that uses a carafe and does not maintain surface heat uses 1 watt per hour when not in use.

Overall, I found that many of the smaller things that consume minor amounts of power cost an average of $2.10 a year to operate at 12 cents per kWh (e.g., 2 watts wasted = 2 watts x 24 hrs x 365 days = 17,520 watt hrs / 1000 = 17.52 kWh per year x .12 per kWh = $2.10). With this being the case, you could unplug these items if you wish, but you don't need to purchase any special energy-saving devices for these items individually, since the amount of energy consumed to create the energy-saving device will easily exceed what your item may use over several years.

A solution for "energy vampires" would be to relocate them and place them all on one special power strip. This is often not practical, but if you could place all your charger items in one place, then, with each item wasting about $2 each year in power, you'd save enough in a year or two to validate the power consumed to both create and purchase the power strip.

In most cases where you are looking for practical reasons for saving energy, it's not until you hit items that are wasting at least 7 watts per hour that you can justify any extra expense to save energy.

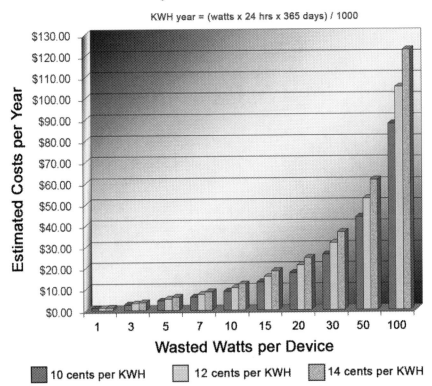

Yearly Cost for Wasted Watts

KWH year = (watts x 24 hrs x 365 days) / 1000

For any item, large or small, you can easily save power, at no cost to you, by simply changing your habits and unplugging things you rarely use or unplugging things when you are finished using them.

To get a better handle on how much any watt level will cost in a years time, review our **Yearly Costs for Wasted Watts** chart, which indicates yearly costs from 1 to 100 watts of power at ten cents, twelve cents, and fourteen cents per kWh. This chart assumes the item is always plugged in and does not account for when the item is actually in use, so the actual "wasted amounts" may be slightly lower.

Reducing Wasted Computer Power Costs

Studies have shown that the average computer's idle time represents from 69 to 97 percent of its total annual energy use, regardless of whether power management software is utilized.

Much of this waste is very avoidable, since many of us have adopted the habit of simply leaving the computer running for hours or even days when we are not even using it. Perhaps we have been working on a project and just do not want to go through the saving and shut-down process, or we simply forget the computer is running, but regardless of our reasons, our computer, monitor, printer, sound system, external drives, scanners, and other peripheral devices sit quietly in the background, consuming power, even if we do not use them for days.

To put things into perspective, I hooked up a ***Kill-A-Watt***[2] metering device in line with the main power that supplies my entire computer system, so that I might determine what my system draws while under normal use. My results were:

- With the computer turned on and all peripherals activated, the system consumes an average of 171 watts per hour, which is equivalent to having thirteen 60-watt-equivalent CFL-powered lamps turned on for that same period of time.

- With the computer turned off, but all peripherals still activated, the watt readings on the Kill-A-Watt meter dropped to 52 watts per hour.

- With all peripherals turned off manually, I ended up with a final reading of 16 watts per hour, which was being used by my *UPS* (uninterruptible power supply*)*, which is the one thing that must maintain a charge.

With this data in mind, and forming a base of normally using the computer system for eight hours a day, let's look at both the typical level of waste when we leave peripheral devices running when not in use and also the extreme level of energy waste when we leave the computer running when not in use.

Typical Example: When we've shut down the computer after its eight hours of normal use, the remaining components still use 52 watts of power per hour. Since my UPS uses 16 watts per hour and needs to stay on, the power wasted by the peripherals in the background is 36 watts per hour. This is nearly equivalent to having three 13-watt CFL-powered lamps turned on for an hour.

If the system is normally inactive for the remaining 16 hours of the day, the average waste for the year by leaving the peripheral devices running would be 36 watts x 16 hours x 365 days = 210,240 watts per year. We divide this by 1000 to get 210.24 kWh (kilowatt hours). At 14 cents per kWh, a yearly waste of $29.43 would be realized.

Extreme Example: If, after using the computer system for the average eight-hour period of the day, you failed to shut down the entire computer system half the time, the total wasted power and associated costs would be: 171 total watts - 16 watts used by UPS = 155 wasted watts x 16 hours x 182 days = 451,360 watts. We divide this by 1000 to get a total of 451.4 kilowatt hours wasted by leaving your computer system on half of the time when you should have shut it down.

Meanwhile, even when the computer system was turned off, if the peripherals are not shut off as portrayed in the previous example, we add 105 kWh, which is half the total of kWh from the "typical example" detailed above, for a total of 556.52 wasted kWh. At 14 cents per kWh, a yearly waste of $77.91 would be realized.

Bear in mind that these examples are only for one computer and can be multiplied for the number of computers you have in your home.

Since we all love using our computers, that power is normally well used, but to waste power with our computers is totally unnecessary and can be fixed by doing two things:

1. Pick up an ***Energy Saving Smart Strip***[3] that monitors when your computer is running and detects when you shut it off. This device then automatically shuts down all your peripheral devices. The Energy Saving Smart Strip costs about $39 and will easily pay for itself within a year or two.

2. Turn the computer off each night or when you are finished with it. Make it a point to at least turn the computer off, knowing that the smart strip will take care of other things for you automatically.

More Ways to Cut Back Computer Energy Costs

Replace tube-style *CRT monitors* with *LCD monitors* to save power:

- Even if it's only on for eight hours a day, seven days a week, the average yearly cost for a CRT monitor that uses about 84 watts of power can be calculated with the following formula: ((84 watts x 8 hrs a day x 365 days a year) / 1000 hours) x .14 cents per kWh = $34.33 for its yearly energy costs. Meanwhile, with an average LCD display only using 35 watts of power, the formula would be: ((35 watts x 8 hrs a day x 365 days a year) / 1000 hours) x .14 cents per kWh = $14.30 for its yearly energy costs, for a total savings of $20.03 per year.

Blank your screen vs. turning off monitor displays:

- LCD displays can go "black" when you shut them off or you turn all pixels to black. While both choices result in a black display, just setting the background to black saves absolutely nothing, while turning it off results in significant energy savings. To truly cut back the amount of power consumed by your monitor, you should avoid screen savers and turn the monitor off instead. If using Windows, simply set the screen saver activation time longer than the Monitor Power time in the Display Properties control panel.

Give your hard drives a rest:

- Set your hard drives to "sleep" during inactivity. You can set this via the Control Panel, under the Power Options section. This is particularly helpful if you have more than one drive on your machine, since each hard drive consumes from 3 to 5 watts.

Saving Power through Recycling and Waste Awareness

Recycling on a residential scale generally consists of segregating your plastic bottles, aluminum cans, glass jars, newspapers, and tin cans from the rest of your everyday garbage. Although you may be aware that this helps reduce landfill problems, you might not be aware how this process saves you money.

The price of everything you buy is affected by the costs that manufacturers and distributors pay for the raw materials to create a product and by the supplies and equipment necessary to package and ship the product. By recycling, you help to reduce these overall costs, which results in lower costs for the products you purchase.

The process to recover and reuse the plastic in a discarded drinking bottle or aluminum can uses many times less the amount of power and resources than the process to initially obtain the resources from the earth and process them for first use.

Most cities and large suburban areas enforce mandatory recycling, so you will be helping the environment and saving energy whether you have really chosen to or not. For those of you living in more secluded areas, however, where mandatory recycling is not enforced, a little more effort and commitment may be necessary to perform your recycling.

Whether recycling is mandatory or not, you can take even further steps to be more environmentally friendly and save money that does end up in your pocket. Here are some ideas to consider:

Instead of buying those cases of drinking water, purchase a water purifier that either fits on your faucet or is part of a water pitcher. Follow up by purchasing a stainless steel or aluminum drinking bottle with a cap. Now, instead of buying case after case of bottled water, which leaves a lot of plastic to recycle, fill your personal water bottle with your own purified water and save yourself hundreds of dollars each year by not buying water—which costs almost nothing right out of the tap.

Canned vegetables may seem convenient, but frozen vegetables taste so much better, include a greater amount of vitamins, and last almost forever when kept frozen. Unlike with canned versions, it's easy to use small portions to add to soups or individual dinner servings, plus there is no can to recycle.

If you drink lots of soda, you can save much money and reduce your volume of recyclables by purchasing soda in large bottles rather than six-packs and cases of bottles or cans. One large bottle of soda costs less than the equivalent amount in multiple smaller containers, plus one large container crushes easier and takes up less space in your recycling bin than a dozen smaller cans or bottles.

Laundry detergent bottles take up a lot of space and are almost impossible to crush when you place them in your recycling bin. To ease this problem, look for the newer detergents from Era or Tide that are highly concentrated. You will pay less per load and will have a smaller bottle later when it's time to recycle.

If you do prefer to buy beverages that use aluminum cans, purchase a 12-ounce can crusher to significantly reduce the amount of necessary recycling space. If you produce a lot of cans, you can go even one step further and save these cans separately from your recyclables. After you fill one or more 30-gallon garbage bags, take them to your local scrap yard and get cold, hard cash for your efforts.

Overall, everyone wins when you recycle or become more aware of what you are using, so that you decrease the level of what must be recycled. Every effort you make reduces power consumption and improves the world we live in.

....

Resources:

1 Dryer Vent Seal: http://www.energyefficientchoices.com/products/besp/dryer-vent-seal.html

2 Kill-A-Watt: http://www.energyefficientchoices.com/products/kill-a-watt-meter.html

3 Energy Saving Smart Strip: http://www.energyefficientchoices.com/products/energy-saving-smart-strip.html

2

The Best Methods for Heating and Cooling

Our heating and cooling needs far exceed what we may require for basic lighting and appliance use, so even a small improvement with heating and cooling efficiencies can add up to substantial savings.

Some factors that cannot be resolved by selecting the best heating or cooling system have to do with how efficiently and effectively your home is built to retain the conditioned air.

If you are building a new home, there will be very little issue with ensuring there is sufficient insulating and proper door and window seals, but if you are simply looking to replace an antiquated heating or cooling system in your older home, be sure to also budget for adding a layer of insulation to the attic and upgrading your doors and windows.

Any expenses from improvements you make may provide immediate benefits, since they can quite possibly allow you to install a smaller heating or cooling unit. This is especially true in older homes, where a massive coal furnace and huge radiators were necessary to heat the original home that had no insulation at all and had no real seals on doors or windows.

In many cases, it's very probable that some heat-saving improvements have been made in the past, and, as a direct result, it's quite possible that the existing heating system is currently oversized.

When replacing any heating system, don't size the replacement system based upon what is currently installed. First, make all the additional improvements you can, and then have a fresh heating and cooling load calculation performed on the home by a professional heating contractor or technician. Then, based upon the revised heating and cooling load, install your new heating and cooling system.

If you make an adjustment of more than 20 percent of the previous system size, you may also find it necessary to update system pipe sizes, radiator sizes, or duct sizes to more evenly move your conditioned air or hot water throughout your home.

The Most Efficient Method for Heating and Cooling Your Home

One of my goals is to help you to decide against the use of less efficient fossil fuels for heating and cooling your home, so that you are not so increasingly affected by the demand or fear of oil and gas availability as each decade passes.

With most fossil fuels providing an average of only 85 to 90 percent fuel efficiency, this means that 10 to 15 percent of what you pay to heat your home goes right up the chimney. This *chimney effect* is often sucking out the warm air that has been heated, and it requires a lot of unconditioned air to infiltrate into your home, further reducing the efficiency of the heating system.

The only true energy choice, if you wish to eliminate the need for fossil fuel combustion in your home for heating, is to utilize clean, readily available *electricity*. Since this is also the form of energy used for most cooling applications, you simply need to set aside any preconceived notions that heating should only be obtained through fossil fuels. This same process of new thinking was also necessary for the early users of natural gas air conditioning. Eventually, electricity proved to be the better choice.

In its raw use as *electric resistance heat*, electricity is 99.9 percent efficient, but at a time when fossil fuels were cheap, electricity was clearly the most expensive method you could select to heat your home.

Back then, had I suggested you replace your oil or gas heating system with an electric system, you would assume I was misinformed or simply ignorant of true heating costs, but times have truly changed now that fossil fuel prices have been proven to often rise in dramatic stages.

One argument, when talking about using electricity to heat your home or even to run your car, is that since the power companies may be burning coal to make your electricity, you are not really helping the environment at all. This could not be any further from the truth.

The fact is that when a power plant is burning coal, it is burning this fuel at much higher efficiencies than you could possibly expect from a residential furnace, plus these massive power plants incorporate chimney scrubbers and all forms of filtering efforts to significantly reduce the amount of soot and ash that enters the atmosphere. Your home chimney does not do that at all.

You also have to consider that 20 percent of our nation's electricity is created by nuclear power, which has no measurable carbon footprint, plus there is an increasing amount of power being provided by wind farms, solar farms, and hydroelectricity. So yes, *choosing electricity as your fuel source is the most economical and greenest choice you could make.*

Another factor when selecting a heating source is its associated maintenance. Oil and coal furnaces for example, require yearly cleaning and tune-ups. They also make it necessary for your chimney to be cleaned every few years, plus they have the potential to break down more often due to soot or high-heat related issues.

On the other hand, when heating with electricity, the level of maintenance and the wear and tear on equipment is minimal and adds from very little to nothing to your yearly budget. Electricity has also maintained a much more stable price structure and is not likely to simply double in price from one quarter to the next as happens with some fossil fuels such as oil and propane gas.

Using Electricity to Heat with a Heat Pump

One of the greatest innovations of the past fifty years, which set the stage for making electricity the optimum choice for heating, was the development of the *heat pump*.

What is a heat pump? Basically, a heat pump is an air conditioner than can run in reverse. During the heat pump cooling cycle, it absorbs the heat inside your home and exhausts it outside. During the heat pump heating cycle, it absorbs the heat outside the home and exhausts it inside. What makes a heat pump so unusual is that it can find heat in outside air, even when the air temperature is close to 10 degrees F or -12 degrees C.

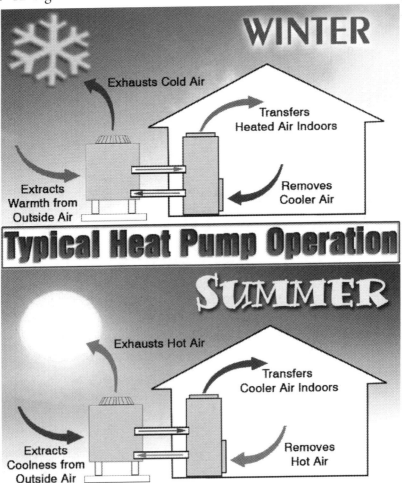

A heat pump uses electricity to provide heat, but instead of simply providing 1 kW of heat by burning 1 kW of electricity, a heat pump extracts free heat energy that is normally not accessible from either the air or the ground. The heat pump collects this heat and focuses it, so that the heat pump outputs more heat than what electricity alone would have provided. In essence, a heat pump uses power to gather heat that is freely available—thus it provides more heat than the power it initially consumes.

Heat pump technology should not be confused with the concept of *perpetual motion* where you create more energy than existed, because that's not possible. There is a universal law which states you can neither create nor destroy energy but can only change it from one form to another. Heat pumps follow this principal as they gather together billions of little heat particles that we normally can not detect and then group them all together for us in a way we do notice. In essence, it can be said that heat pumps recycle heat we had considered unusable, which really makes this form of heating very green.

The extent of how much extra heat is absorbed from the outside air is called the COP or Coefficient of Performance. A good heat pump that has a COP of 2.5 means that the heat pump attracts or gathers together 2.5 times the amount of heat that would normally have been supplied by using electric resistance heating alone.

A more current method of rating a heat pump is by its HSPF (Heating Seasonal Performance Factor). This rating system takes into consideration that the heat pump will run during parts of spring and fall as well, when temperatures are above winter design temperatures.

To ascertain a heat pump's efficiency level using its HSPF rating, simply divide the rated HSPF by 3.414, which is the number of watts in a BTU, and then multiply the result by 100 to obtain a percentage value. For example, a heat pump with a HSPF of 8.2 would have an efficiency rating of 8.2 / 3.414 = 2.4 x 100 = 240%. This simply states that this heat pump can provide 240% more heat than what electricity alone could have provided.

It doesn't take a math wizard to see how you could immediately decrease your heating costs by half or more had you previously heated with electric baseboard heat. Likewise, as shown in the Heating Fuel Cost Comparison Calculator, you can see the differences in the cost to heat a typical home using oil, natural gas, electricity, propane gas, or coal. You can easily see that using electricity along with the heat pump provides the lowest average heating costs for homes.

A final consideration when choosing to change from your favorite fossil fuel to electricity is yearly maintenance costs. Heat pumps will work best if serviced twice per year as the winter and summer seasons approach. You could expect to pay about sixty dollars a visit.

HEATING FUEL COST COMPARISON CALCULATOR

Sq Ft of Home:			1500
Avg Htg BTUH Sq Ft:			30
Heating Load:			45,000

Fuel Type	Fuel Unit	Fuel Price Per Unit (dollars)	Fuel Heat Content Per Unit (Btu)	Heating Appliance Type	Type of Eff. Rating	Eff. Rating	Approx. Eff. (%)	Current Fuel Cost Per Year
Fuel Oil (#2)	Gallon	$3.60	138,690	Furnace or Boiler	AFUE	78.0	78%	$2,536.81
Electricity	KWH	$0.110	3,412	Furnace or Boiler	Estimate	95.0	95%	$2,586.94
				Air-Source Heat Pump 5	HSPF	8.0	234%	$1,048.16
				Heat Pump Boiler	HSPF	11.0	322%	$762.30
				Geothermal Heat Pump	HSPF	11.5	337%	$729.16
				Baseboard/Room Heater	Estimate	100.0	100%	$2,457.59
Natural Gas	Therm	$1.59	100,000	Furnace or Boiler	AFUE	80.0	80%	$1,515.07
				Room Heater (Vented)	AFUE	65.0	65%	$1,864.70
				Room Heater (Unvented)	Estimate	100.0	100%	$1,287.15
Propane	Gallon	$2.75	91,333	Furnace or Boiler	AFUE	80.0	80%	$2,869.07
				Room Heater (Vented)	AFUE	65.0	65%	$3,531.16
Coal	Ton	$200.00	21,910,000	Furnace/Boiler/Stove	Estimate	75.0	75%	$927.80

Price Sources:

Oil	http://tonto.eia.doe.gov/dnav/pet/pet_pri_dist_a_EPD2_PRT_cpgal_m.htm
Electricity	http://www.eia.doe.gov/cneaf/electricity/epm/table5_6_b.html
Natural Gas	http://tonto.eia.doe.gov/dnav/ng/ng_pri_sum_a_EPG0_PRS_DMcf_m.htm
Propane	http://tonto.eia.doe.gov/dnav/pet/pet_pri_prop_a_EPLLPA_PRT_cpgal_m.htm
Coal	Check Local Listings

Alternately, with oil or coal a yearly cleaning is necessary, at an approximate cost of sixty dollars. Additional costs include chimney cleaning every three years for about one hundred dollars. These furnaces also experience much higher occurrences of winter breakdowns due to soot buildup and the extremes of heat. To be safe, you should budget for at least one emergency call per year at an average cost of ninety dollars plus parts.

If you do not already have a heat pump system, I highly recommend that you hire a professional heat pump installer to provide you with a serious evaluation and estimate. Your savings could be substantial, and you will have made a very green decision.

Types of Heat Pump Systems

Geothermal Heat Pumps. Geothermal heat pumps draw heat from the ground or from groundwater. This provides a very consistent temperature throughout all seasons of the year, from which it can withdraw heat or expel heat. This style of heat pump requires much more planning to install and is generally easier to put in place with new construction than retrofitting an existing heating system, since it does require some form of excavating or drilling.

For heating purposes, a geothermal heat pump has a consistent ground temperature to work with that rarely drops below 45 degrees F or 20 degrees C. This allows it to provide a steady COP (coefficient of performance) of around 3.5 to 4. What this means is that for every kWh of electricity it consumes, it provides three to four times that amount in actual heat.

Right now, there is no more efficient heating method available than geothermal, since you are virtually absorbing the heat stored within the planet, and this heat is freely available, releases no gases, and will not run out for another billion years or so. It's the greenest, safest, and most stable source of heat that exists.

Air Source Heat Pumps. Air source heat pumps use the outside air as their heat-absorbing source. This style of heat pump is generally easy to install and is not very expensive. Since most new homes are generally outfitted with air conditioning by default, the air source heat pump provides a heating source while adding very little additional cost to the home's construction.

For heating purposes, air source heat pumps with an HSPF rating of 8.5 or more generally only work well at temperatures above 20 degrees F or 5 degrees C. This means that for every kWh of electricity the heat pump consumes, it provides at least twice that amount in home heating capacity (8.5 HSPF / 3.414=2.50) until temperatures drop well below freezing.

Once temperatures drop below the heat pump's capacity to adequately provide heat for the home, a backup heat source, such as electric resistance heat, is necessary to help maintain the home's proper temperature. This is where heat pumps had previously gotten a bad rap, especially in colder northern climates.

Good news with respect to air source heats pumps is the growing development of extremely high-efficiency heat pumps. One such heat pump, *Trane's*[1] XL19i (photo courtesy of Trane), provides a HSPF of 8.9 and a SEER (seasonal energy-efficiency rating) of 17.9, resulting in an efficiency level of 260% at temperatures well below freezing.

Although it's not likely that air source heat pumps will ever provide efficiency levels that match or beat those of geothermal heat pumps, the differences are thinning. As air source heat pumps continue to provide even greater amounts of heat at lower outdoor temperatures, their lower installation costs work well to truly make them a more practical home heating choice.

Overall, the growing improvements in the efficiency levels of air source heat pumps is good news for most individuals who wish to depend upon their heat pumps in cold climates but do not have the land space or geology that would allow for the installation of anything but an air source heat pump.

Primary Advantages of Choosing a Heat Pump

There is an Unlimited Source of Power. You can't drill for your own oil or gas, and you can't dig up your own coal (in most cases), but you can make choices to either create or use power from sources that are unlimited and have absolutely no impact on our environment. These power sources currently consist of solar, wind, and hydroelectric. When using a heat pump that draws power from one of these resources, your power source is unlimited and creates no carbon footprint.

You Gain Access to Free Heat. The reason a heat pump works so well for heating is that it extracts heat from the air, ground, or water (depending upon your system), and this portion of your heat is absolutely free! Your only cost is the small amount of power necessary for the heat pump scroll compressor to gather that heat together and transfer it to your home. If fossil fuels worked the same way, you would only pay for the fuel to be delivered to your home, but the fuel itself would be free.

Your Health is Not Affected. Using electricity via a heat pump to heat your home eliminates fossil fuels from your home. This means there is no possibility of carbon monoxide poisoning, plus there is nothing in your home that is consuming the oxygen that you need to live a happy and healthy life.

Heat is Not Wasted. All fossil fuels require venting to the outdoors and/or a fresh air intake to compensate for the oxygen they deplete and the gases they release. This means that air must be drawn into your home so that it can be exhausted out. Some gas and oil furnaces provide a closed loop for this, but most simply exhaust the air up the chimney, which forces frigid air to be sucked in from other areas of the house. If air is being pushed out, then it is also being sucked in through small cracks around windows, door frames, or poorly constructed walls. This is called *infiltration,* but is generally referred to as *drafts.* Heat pumps require no fresh air to be drawn into the home, and, therefore, they do not suck in frigid air and then toss your heated air away.

To summarize: Heat pump technology allows you to use electricity in an extremely efficient manner, which results in your heating costs being reduced by half or more, while also improving your home's state of health and reducing your carbon footprint on the planet's atmosphere.

Tips for Reducing Your Heating and Cooling Demand

Here are a few tips that will help reduce the load on your heating and cooling systems so that they do not have to work so hard; this will result in further reductions of your heating and cooling costs.

Insulating and Sealing. In the summer, the attic is the first layer of defense between your home's living space and the sun. In the winter, the attic is the final layer between your heated air and the frigid air outdoors. The most economical thing you can do is to add layers of insulation to your attic or have more insulation blown in.

As insulation ages and compacts its R-value drops, so even if your home was insulated well when it was built thirty to forty years ago, it needs to be topped off to compensate for natural compression and also to make up for the fact that construction standards may have been lower at the time the home was built.

For the winter, if you have older windows, seal the windows with plastic, either from weatherization kits that are readily available or by simply cutting plastic sheets and securing them with duct tape. Also, add weather stripping to doors, and replace screens with storm windows, or cover the screens with plastic.

Attic Ventilation. During the summer, your attic crawl space can easily exceed 130 degrees. Proper venting, such as installing a ridge vent, can be helpful in allowing the heat at the attic's highest level to more easily escape.

If you have chosen to add more insulation to your attic space, check to make sure none of your eaves are blocked and that your attic still has airflow from each eave to the ridge vent.

Another great ventilation aid is to install a ***solar-powered exhaust vent***[2] that only turns on at high temperature and uses only the power of the sun to provide this extra ventilation. Since there is no wiring necessary, any basic carpenter or handyman can install this form of vent.

Exhaust Systems. Your bathroom fans, stovetop fans, and clothes dryer are all items that exhaust your heated or cooled air outside, requiring air to be drawn in from the outside, resulting in hot, humid air or cold, frigid air being sucked into your home when you least desire it.

Do not use your clothes dryer on extreme temperature days, such as summer days at 90 degrees and greater or on winter days at 20 degrees or lower. In the summer, the heat of the day peaks between 3:00 PM and 6:00 PM, so run your dryer earlier in the morning or much later at night. Likewise, in the winter, the night temperatures may be frigid and drop into the single digits. Run your clothes dryer only during the afternoon and early evening, when the air is the warmest of the day.

For your bathroom exhaust fans, replace the simple on/off switch with a timed switching device of no more than sixty minutes. It is necessary to ventilate the bathroom, but it's totally wasteful to run the exhaust fan all day while you are at work, exhausting your heated air outside. You might as well have just left a window open all day.

During the winter, use your stovetop exhaust fan only if you have actual smoke to exhaust. Do not use it to exhaust steam, since your home already lacks moisture in the winter, and the steam will perform no harm and will actually improve breathing conditions in the home. In the summer, this line of thinking is reversed, since you definitely do want to exhaust the steam. So, in the summer be sure to run the fans to exhaust the steam and smoke, and do your best to remember to turn them off when not in use.

Free Heating and Cooling. Depending upon your geographic location and the position your home faces, you can take advantage of windows and curtains to add or block heat, depending upon the time of year. In the winter, allow the sun to enter your southern windows during the day, but in the summer, be sure to keeps those blinds drawn.

For summer cooling, install a whole-house exhaust system and run it on nights when the outdoor temperature drops. Simply turn the unit on, open your windows, and allow the house to cool off naturally, with just a little help from one central fan.

If you have enough land available, plant evergreens on the north/northwest side of your home. In time, these trees will shield your home from the cold winter winds and will also provide summer shade from the late afternoon and evening sun.

Temperature Settings. If you raise or lower the temperature settings too much in order to save energy it can become uncomfortable in your home, and that can only lead to associating energy efficiency with something that is undesirable—and then you might stop being efficient altogether.

Heating systems are generally designed to provide your home with the capacity to maintain 70 degrees indoors when it's zero degrees outdoors. By eliminating drafts and simply wearing long-sleeve shirts and socks during the winter, you can easily reduce your home's temperature setting to 65 degrees and be totally comfortable. Any lower than that and you may start feeling uncomfortable.

Cooling systems are generally designed to provide your home with the capacity to maintain 75 degrees indoors when it's 95 degrees outdoors. Since the main discomfort issue in the summer is humidity, you can be comfortable in your home at higher temperatures, since the home's humidity levels are reduced when the air conditioner is running. By eliminating unnecessary exhaust and door openings and closings, you could increase your home's temperature setting to 78 or 80 degrees and be totally comfortable if you dress lightly and keep drapes drawn that favor the sunny side of your home.

For either heating or cooling, you can alter the temperature settings from 5 to 10 degrees when you are not going to be at home for eight to twelve hours. Making an alteration of any greater amount only leads to your system overworking to recover, and this is inefficient. If you are going to be away for days, you can reduce the heating to 55 degrees or raise the cooling temperature to 90 degrees, and this will prevent freezing or baking issues.

You can also install a programmable thermostat to better define the periods when you plan to be home or not, plus you can also set winter heating temperatures lower during the night when you are sleeping and have them bump back up a few degrees a half hour before you awake.

Note: I find that many individuals turn off their central air conditioning when not at home and then they will often return to their sweltering home later that day. In the same way that you would not turn off your heat, don't turn off the air conditioning if you are returning later that day. Instead, set the thermostat to 90 degrees and allow it to maintain that temperature, so that the unit does not have to work so hard to remove all the moisture and humidity at day's end when the outdoor temperatures are excessive and outdoor humidity levels have peaked.

Resources:

[1] Trane: http://www.trane.com

[2] solar powered exhaust vent: http://www.energyefficientchoices.com/ products/besp/solar-powered-exhaust-vent.html

3

Creating Hot Water Efficiently

Next to heating and cooling, the second-largest consumption of energy in the home is due to the creation and storage of hot water for showers, baths, laundry, and dishes.

Until recently, the most efficient method you could possibly use to create hot water was by using tankless water heaters that ran primarily on natural gas or propane. With these heaters, water is instantly heated to temperature only as it is needed. Their great benefit is that no water is stored, so there is very little waste.

Electric water heaters have been around for a long time, but their expense to operate was often much higher than that of cheaper fossil fuels such as natural gas or oil. In addition, electric water heaters had long *recovery rates*, which resulted in a hot shower for the first person and a gradually colder shower for anyone who immediately followed.

These heaters often got installed due to cheaper installation costs or simply because no other fuel source was readily available. For most homeowners who had electric water heaters, the overall feeling was that they were stuck with heating water in the most expensive way possible.

New Electric Water Heating Options

Innovation and necessity have led to great improvements in using electricity to heat water. Several options now exist that rival what we previously thought only fossil fuels could do.

Heat Pump Water Heaters

Yes, that's right, a water heater that gets its heat from thin air, so to speak. Heat pumps gain their efficiency by using electricity to gather and move heat instead of using electricity to simply create heat directly through the use of electrical resistance heating elements.

Using the same heat pump principles as with extracting outdoor heat to heat your home, heat pump water heaters extract heat from the outside air and use this energy to heat your water. Since heat pump water heaters extract heat from the air, they deliver about twice the heat at half the price of a conventional electric water heater, resulting in reduced heating costs of 25 percent or more.

Although you can purchase the entire heat pump water heater as one unit, I like the retrofit version best, since it allows for easy conversion for anyone with an existing electric water heater. ***E-Teck residential high-efficiency heat pump water heaters***[1] can easily be added to the top of most electric water heaters with minimal electrical and plumbing modifications. (Photo courtesy of E-Teck.)

A really nice side effect of heat pump water heaters is that they also dehumidify the space in which they are located. This is a great saving for water heaters in basements where you already have a dehumidifier running. Now your savings go beyond what you saved on heating water alone and extend to not having to run a separate dehumidifier.

If you do not require the dehumidification feature, most heat pump water heaters also provide the option to simply vent the cooler air outdoors.

For styles that depend upon outside air temperature, their performance will vary, and the amount of heat available will drop as the outside temperature goes below freezing.

While this style of heat pump will normally work fine for nonfrigid climates, if you live in a northern climate I recommend that you use the heat pump water heater as a preheater to an electric water heating device and not as a stand-alone unit. By doing this, you will reap the great benefit of creating lower-cost hot water, but you will not lose your capacity to have sufficient hot water whenever you need it, no matter how cold it gets outside.

For styles that work on the heat available within your confined garage or basement space, outdoor temperature issues do not matter, and this unit can simply be viewed as a dehumidifier that also heats or preheats your water.

Another factor to consider is the hot water *recovery rate*. This is the amount of water the heater can bring up to the desired temperature during a one-hour period. Today's heat pump water heaters provide about fifteen gallons per hour of hot water. In contrast, a typical electric water heater has a recovery rate of about twenty gallons per hour, and a gas water heater has a recovery rate of about thirty-five gallons per hour.

With this in mind, depending upon the size of your family and your specific hot water needs, we suggest that the average size family use heat pump water heaters in conjunction with your existing electric water heater or solar water heater.

Tankless Electric Water Heaters

Electric resistance heating finally makes a comeback with the water heater that does not spend any energy maintaining the temperature of a holding tank.

In terms of initial product cost, electric tankless water heaters cost significantly less than their gas counterparts. Whole-house electric tankless water heaters cost about U.S. $400–700, while gas tankless water heaters generally cost U.S. $1,000 or more, especially for better quality systems with electronic ignition systems.

Tankless electric water heaters[2] are 98+ percent efficient, have a longer service life, and are cheaper to install than comparable gas units. Inasmuch as gas prices tend to fluctuate more dramatically then electricity prices, we can expect gas prices to rise at a higher and faster rate than electricity prices.

To make use of a tankless electric water heater, you need the minimum of a 200-amp service in your home, since the electric tankless water heater draws a considerable amount of power during its short-term use cycles.

While a standard electric heater may only require one 240 V 30-amp circuit, the average tankless electric water heater requires two 240 V 60-amp circuits. This is necessary so that it can provide endless hot water without having to store a drop.

Benefits:

- Reduces your energy costs from 15 to 20 percent compared to standard electric water heaters.

- It's a very green choice when compared to standard water heaters, since it uses fewer resources to be manufactured, uses less power when running, and is much more easily recycled after its lifetime has expired.

- There is no need for a chimney or exhaust system, which is a necessity for all tankless gas water heating systems. This also means no unnecessary outside air is being drawn into your home, and no danger of carbon monoxide poisoning exists.

Solar Water Heating Options

During each day, the almost infinite energy of the sun is sitting right above you, and depending upon your geographic location and typical weather conditions, your home water heating solution could very well be provided through solar energy.

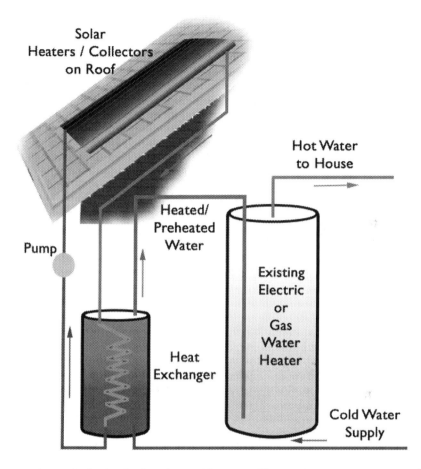

A typical single-family residence will require one or two solar collector panels on the roof. These panels resemble skylights, and are about four feet wide and eight feet long.

With most solar water heating systems, when the collector panels on your roof are heated by the sun, hot water or a heat transfer liquid circulates from them to a storage tank that is separate from your existing water heater. The cold water supply goes to the solar storage tank first, and is either preheated or fully heated before it passes into your existing water heater.

The end result of installing a solar water heating system is that your existing water heater will run about 70 percent less than it did in the past, since the water supply is being preheated before it even gets to your existing water heater.

Is It Right for You?

To determine if this form of system could work for you, you'll need to confirm whether your roof has a southern exposure that is not shaded by trees or nearby structures.

Then you'll want to determine the amount of solar energy that is available to you, given your geographic location. The quickest way to do this is to get a ***Solar Estimate***[3], which can be calculated for hot water, for electrical (PV), or spa/pool heating.

You'll want to take note of your estimated *solar rating per sq/m* a day, which is useful information for sizing a hot water system, but is also useful knowledge to have on hand if you are looking to add solar power panels for other purposes.

For solar hot water heating purposes, take note of the estimated *solar collector size*. Depending upon which brand of solar water heating system you choose, you'll have a good idea of the system size to focus on.

For example, when using the Solar Estimator, I start by selecting my state, followed by my county. I then select my current power provider (this is not required and is just for the sake of comparison), and then I select the type of system I am interested in sizing, which happens to be hot water. I click on Estimate my Solar System, and I am provided with a wealth of data on sizing, capacity, and even estimated installation costs and payback periods.

In my case, my solar rating is 4.5 kWh per square meter a day, and my estimated hot water heating system solar size is 32.3 square feet, or about six feet by six feet.

Conserving Hot Water

No matter what method you use to heat your water, and no matter how efficient your water heating method may be, you can still improve the overall costs for heating your water by changing a few habits regarding its use.

Hot Water for Showers and Baths

The single greatest use for hot water in the home is for showering and bathing. With the average person taking a ten-minute shower each day and with an average of four people in the home, the average family can easily make use of their hot water heating system for forty minutes or more, just for showers.

Older, nonconserving showerheads can easily allow from 5 to 8 gallons per minute of water flow. By using an average of 6.5 gallons per minute, 260 gallons could be used by family showers each day, with 80%, or 208 gallons, of that being just for hot water.

Water-saving showerheads do not allow more than 2.5 gallons of flow per minute, and I've seen some down as low as 1.6 gallons of water flow per minute. If you are using an older showerhead, the simple act of changing the showerhead(s) can make a major difference in the amount of hot water you consume. You could effectively cut your water use in half or more.

Another issue is with people who take long showers—you know who you are. So, just what is an acceptable amount of time that anyone should use in the shower? There will be variations, but as an overall average, according to ***Moen's***[4] study of bathroom usage, "Most people think they spend up to twenty minutes in the shower, but our research showed people actually shower in ten minutes or less."

With this data in mind, those who find themselves still showering after thirty minutes, forty-five minutes, or even after an hour, can easily make a significant decrease in water use by attempting to join the national norm and cutting their time to no more than fifteen minutes per shower. This will also lead to significant savings on water consumption overall and would be a very green choice to make.

Hot Water for Your Dishwasher

Many older dishwashers required a minimum temperature of 140 degrees in order to properly clean your dishes. Due to many innovative changes in dishwasher design and dishwasher detergent cleansing power, all energy-efficient or Energy Star-rated dishwashers work fine at hot water temperatures of 120 degrees or less.

If you replaced your dishwasher in the past few years, check the manufacturer's instructions to confirm its required hot water design level. If the required setting is 120 degrees or lower, be sure to check your water heater settings and lower the temperature setting to 120 degrees.

If your dishwasher is seven years old or older, you can save a significant amount of energy by replacing it now. Modern dishwashers allow lower input temperature water and even use less of it. Many now include booster heaters of their own, so that you don't have to keep your water heating settings high for the whole house just for when you might wash dishes.

Point-of-Use Hot Water

If you have an often-used lavatory or powder room that is located quite some distance from your water heating source, you might benefit from installing a point-of-use water heater for that sink location.

Each time you turn on a hot water faucet to wash your hands or to brush your teeth, etc., a lot of hot water can easily be wasted if it's taking more than five seconds for your water to get hot. After you finish washing, all the piping between the water heater and that distance faucet is totally wasted, as it gradually dissipates its heat to the basement or crawl space.

By installing a small water-heating device that fits right under the sink, you'll have instant hot water and will neither waste water while waiting for its temperature to increase, nor will you waste heated water that is slowly cooling off in one hundred feet of pipe.

Resources:

[1] E-Teck residential high efficiency heat pump water heaters: http://www.aers.com/etech_residential_water_heating.html

[2] Tankless Electric Water Heaters: http://www.energyefficientchoices.com/products/stiebel-tankless-electric-water-heater.html

[3] Solar Estimate: http://www.energyefficientchoices.com/resources/solar-power-sizing-calculator.html

[4] Moen: http://www.moen.com

4

Tapping Renewable Solar and Wind Energy

Solar PV (photovoltaic) energy, along with wind turbine power, has finally evolved to the point where it is practical, affordable, and beneficial enough to seriously consider as a dependable power source for any home or business structure.

Even if renewable energy costs are initially higher than using fossil fuels, solar and wind have one amazing characteristic that just can't be beat. You can be the creator of your own fuel and will not be dramatically affected by unstable fuel costs or feel any pinch when availability of oil or natural gas changes.

In a world driven by the fear of what may change in other countries to affect oil and gas prices, and the resulting surges in prices that often seem to be unjustified, creating your own power, in whole or in part, will provide you with security and peace of mind.

The most exciting aspect of renewable energy at this time is that there are so many innovations in the works which are sure to drop prices dramatically over the next five years. With this in mind, if you find renewable energy too costly to install at this time, you can feel confident that this is sure to change within a few years.

Because of the need for energy independence and due to the variety of home-efficiency products that are finally hitting the shelves, by the year 2015 renewable energy options such as solar, wind, and fuel cells will be much more affordable. At that time, it is more likely that they will be considered as standard fixtures on most new homes and could be more easily added to many existing homes.

The bottom line for most of us is still: "How much will it cost and how quickly will I get my money back?" This is quite understandable, and it's the primary reason this book focuses on finding "practical and affordable answers."

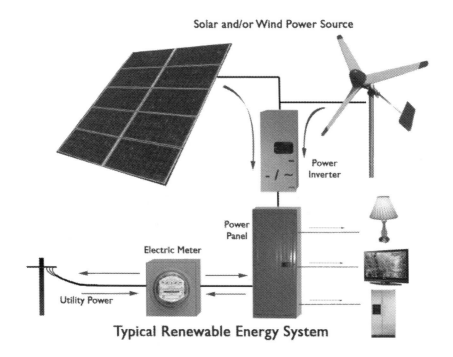

Typical Renewable Energy System

With respect to solar and wind power, the next few sections will show you what you can do today to get the most from renewable energy sources and how you can keep installation prices down as much as possible, thereby reducing the length of time for a return on your investment.

Your choice to create your own clean and renewable energy benefits everyone. Keep this in mind if things appear pricey or if payback periods seem to be too long. The carbon you don't burn and the gases you do not pump into the atmosphere are a benefit to all life, so everyone and all things win when you choose to go green.

Creating your own power also empowers you, because it provides you with security. You will be more at peace knowing your investment in providing your own power has stabilized your monthly energy budget for the rest of your life.

Using Solar Power as a Renewable Energy Source

Solar PV technology has been available for use for over forty years, yet its expense has often had it sitting in the shadows as other forms of power proved to be much cheaper and readily available.

Every time we have an energy crisis in some form or another, many of us look again at solar energy to see if anything has changed to finally justify the expense of installing a solar power system. The answer is— we are getting closer.

Current solar panels average 15 percent efficiency, which means there is still a tremendous amount of room for improvement. Since solar panels and devices have never been in high demand, production levels are generally low, thus keeping production costs high, resulting in high consumer costs for most solar products.

Some recent innovations, such as extremely thin and flexible solar material, have been introduced by a company called ***Nanosolar***[1]. They have performed years of research and development and are working with other manufacturers that will be using their new technology in their products. (Photo courtesy of Nanosolar.)

I will continue to keep my eye on the product lines that are a direct result of Nanosolar technology, because the benefits of eventually getting away from silicon-wafer-based solar cells are substantial. Production costs for ink-based or film-based solar panels are much smaller, plus the panels are lighter and more flexible, and, here's the best part, they would only cost a fraction of the price of current silicon-based solar panels.

Even with current solar panel costs, if you are building a new home or undergoing any major renovation, you should install a solar power system, since its costs would simply get absorbed into your monthly mortgage payment. You might end up with a slightly higher mortgage, but you would have little or no monthly electricity bill.

Once you decide to install the system, whether you are building new or renovating, it's important for you to keep in mind that the optimum location for the solar panels would be on the south/southwest side of the roof or large field. Although direct sunlight is not necessary for the panel to generate solar power, direct sunlight creates the highest form of power, which means that anything, such as trees or tall buildings, that prevents direct sunlight from hitting the panels will significantly affect the panels' ability to provide its optimum output power.

Geographic Location and Solar Efficiencies

The amount of solar energy available to any location is determined by your position on the earth (latitude) and by your common weather conditions. To see a very close estimate of what the available solar energy is for your geographic area, please feel free to use the ***Solar Power Sizing Calculator***[2] at FindSolar.com

For example, the solar rating for Pennsylvania is 4.39 kWh per square meter per day, while the solar rating in Nevada is 6.39 kWh per square meter per day. This is a whopping difference of 50% .

Due to this difference in location, while it would take 750 square feet of roof space (50 feet x 15 feet) for the solar panels to provide half your energy needs in Nevada, it would require 1300 square feet of roof space (87 feet x 15 feet) for the solar panels to provide half your energy needs in Pennsylvania.

This information is not meant to discourage anyone living in a northern climate from selecting solar power, but to simply inform you that it will cost more than what you generally see on TV, since the homes they show are often located in warmer climates.

Other geographic drawbacks in the north are occasional snow cover and shorter winter daylight hours. Solar panels on snow-covered roofs may not be readily accessible for removing snow. This means the snow will have to melt on its own in order for the panels to resume creating power. Since sunlight can penetrate a few inches of snow, you still may get some minor power output, plus the sun's infrared light may also heat the panels slightly, accelerating the melting of the snow cover.

With winter in mind, if you are located in a northern climate and if you have sufficient land available, it would work best to place the panels on a ground-level rack system that rotated and tilted automatically as the sun moves across the horizon. Not only would this greatly improve your efficiency, at any latitude, but it would also place the panels in a position where they are easier to access and clean.

Types of Solar Panels

There are several different types of solar panels available for home power generation.

Monocrystalline. These are the most efficient form of PV panel, providing 15–18 percent efficiency. These panels are also the most expensive, but they are slightly better in low-light conditions than other types of solar panels. Since these panels provide high efficiency levels, they are generally more cost effective in the long run.

Polycrystalline. These are the most common type of PV panels at this time and are 12–14 percent efficient. They are slightly less efficient and less expensive than monocrystalline panels, but once they are combined in a frame with thirty-five or more other cells, the difference in watts per square foot is insignificant.

Amorphous. These solar panels are generally the lowest-cost solar panels on the market. They perform wonderfully in low-light and overcast conditions.

Concentrator Solar Panels. These panels provide maximum solar output by reflecting the sunlight directly to the panel at the best angle. They are one of the most efficient solar panels on the market, using the principals of the magnifying glass to focus light more precisely on the silicon cell, which makes them highly effective in low-light situations or where you do not have the optimum angle toward the sun.

Using Wind Turbine Energy as a Renewable Energy Source

Back in 1979, while still in high school, I recall reading an article about a man who lived in the Midwest who claimed his electricity bill for the entire year was under ten dollars, because he created his own power using a wind turbine. The ten dollars for his electricity bill was later attributed to a few days where he took his wind turbine offline to perform maintenance and had to use his utility company's power.

I was definitely intrigued by this story and used the idea of energy independence to fashion my own concept of an electric car. I later realized my electric car design had many fatal flaws, but my point was not about building an electric car, it was about embracing the concept of being energy independent.

My career has been almost entirely focused on electricity in one form or another, and I know that part of my motivation was that I always viewed electricity as the energy method that would eventually free all of us from bondage created by using fossil fuels—and it all started with a story of a windmill out West.

One of the greatest features of harnessing wind energy is that it has the potential to provide power twenty-four hours a day. If you live in a location where you are on a high mountain range, or are near a coastline, or are located almost anywhere within the central plains of America, your location is a prime candidate for capturing wind energy. To see a very close estimate of what your available wind energy is for your geographic area, please use the ***Wind Energy Sizing Calculator***[3] provided on our Web site.

When viewing any wind map, keep in mind that most residential-scale wind turbines need a minimum average wind speed of 12 mph in order for the turbine to provide some level of consistent and efficient power output.

For home and commercial applications, they are two forms of wind turbines available.

Horizontal Axis Wind Turbine (HAWT)

This form of wind turbine is currently the most common form of wind turbine and works on the same principals as the standard windmill that many farmers use for pumping water.

The HAWT style generally has three or four blades that spin on a horizontally positioned shaft. This type of blade system works best when lifted vertically thirty feet or more above the ground surface, and at least one hundred to two hundred feet horizontally away from any turbulent air caused by wind passing over trees or homes.

Depending upon the size of the HAWTs, they can be installed on single poles that require no additional guide wires, such as the ***Skystream 3.7 by Southwest Windpower***[4], or they can be installed on standard slim towers that will require the use of guide wires and also generate a larger "footprint" on the available land. (Photo courtesy of Southwest Windpower.)

Two benefits of the Skystream HAWT are that the product price is reasonable, and the installation can generally be performed by local contractors. This helps to keep installation costs down. Other than pouring a concrete base, you can easily complete the rest of the work within a day, and you'll start making your own power by evening.

Alternately, the primary benefit of using a slim tower is that it may provide the additional height necessary to help the turbine achieve its greatest potential. This works very well if you are surrounded by tall trees or structures or are within a valley setting. Achieving the extra height helps reduce any turbulence that may otherwise adversely affect the performance of the wind turbine.

Vertical Axis Wind Turbine (VAWT)

This form of wind turbine is based upon a different engineering design, which adds much more versatility to its application and is slowly becoming more popular.

The VAWT style of wind turbine can have from three to twenty blades that spin on a vertically positioned shaft and may look like a hamster's wheel turned on its side.

The primary advantage of the VAWT style is that it is not adversely affected by turbulent *air* currents and actually does better with them. This allows this form of turbine to be installed on rooftops or on towers where rooftops and tree lines are nearby.

Since many newer homes and almost all older homes within city limits have very little land space to work with, the VAWT style is often the only choice, since air turbulence is high in these areas and most HAWT styles would not do well in this environment.

How Your Renewable Power System Ties into Your Home

Whether you are generating your own power through solar or wind, the bottom line is you need to take that energy and convert it into what your home or business can use. There are two ways of doing this, by using either a *Grid-Tie* or *Off-Grid* system. We will define both of them but will focus on the grid-tie system, since this is the most practical system for most homes.

Grid-Tie Renewable Energy Power Systems

A grid-tie or grid-tied system uses a piece of equipment called a *power inverter* to convert your solar- or wind-generated power into the same power type distributed by the electrical utility provider.

Once your power has been converted, it can be easily used within your home—and it can also exit your home by running your electrical meter backward when you make more power than you need, provided your utility company provides *net metering*.

Since each utility company has its own rules and regulations, you must check with them to specifically determine whether they support net metering and whether they will credit your excess electricity at a retail or wholesale price.

You can quickly access the ***Net Metering Policies***[5] of most utility companies at the U.S. Department of Energy's Web site under the primary category of ***Green Power Markets***[5]

The primary benefits of the grid-tie system are:

- You are always connected to your utility company, so, regardless of the amount of wind or solar energy available, you will always have a power source available.

- If your system is oversized, or when you use little of your own power-generating capacity, this excess power is distributed out into the world, and your electrical utility account is credited with this excess electricity.

It's like banking power, but without having to install costly battery storage systems.

- If your system is oversized, and you end up creating more power on average than what you use, this power is then used by others within your utility provider's distribution system. The result is that not only have you reduced your own carbon footprint on the world, but you are helping others to do this as well, since they will be using power you created.

Off-Grid Renewable Energy Power Systems

Off-grid power systems are generally sized and engineered to provide regulated power to an array of high capacity batteries through the use of a charge controller. The batteries are then connected to a power inverter, which transforms the batteries' DC voltage into usable AC voltage for the home.

Off-grid systems generally cost more, since they must provide 100 percent or more of the power necessary, plus they also require the installation and care of batteries. The three primary battery types are:

- Flooded Lead Acid. These are the most cost-effective form of batteries, but they require heavy maintenance, which involves monitoring battery voltage, adding distilled water, and equalizing the charge. These batteries may also vent hydrogen when charging, so it is recommended that they be stored in a well-ventilated space.

- Sealed Absorbed Glass Mat (AGM). These batteries do not require maintenance, since they are sealed. This also reduces venting to almost immeasurable levels.

- Sealed Gel Cell. These batteries are more costly and have increased sensitivity to overcharging. They too are well sealed, and neither require maintenance, nor do they vent gases; however, they are among the most expensive types of batteries.

The main benefits of off-grid systems are:

- No utility power is required, so this form of system is perfect for remote locations such as cabins, camping areas, or for home locations where no utilities are present.

- You will tend to be as efficient as possible, since there is no alternate power supply.

Benefits of Using Renewable Energy

Fossil fuels were a cheap energy source that ran our homes and industries, but the side effects have been proven to be deadly. Now it's time to consider the benefits of using renewable energy to power the world.

Short of living off the grid and providing 100 percent of all your own energy resources, you can now participate with most utility companies in net metering. This system is designed for homeowners who generate some, or all, of their own power but choose to remain connected to the electrical grid.

With net metering, your electrical utility company provides the means that allows you to sell them your unused electricity, or provide you with credit that you may use in the future at no cost. This is a wonderful system, because it eliminates your need to install costly battery systems to store extra power your house does not consume when the wind-powered generator or solar panel creates it.

For example, if you have little or no electrical demand from your home while your solar panels or wind turbine are chugging away, this power gets sent outside your home, right into the power lines where you normally draw power in. At this time, your meter actually runs backward. At a later time, when the needs of your home exceed the amount of power being generated by your renewable power source, you resume drawing in power from the electrical utility.

Rather than having net metering available, you could store your excess power in a collection of batteries, where it remains available until your power output falls below the level of the needs of your home. At that time the batteries would supply your power, and when they discharged completely, you would automatically resume drawing power in from your electricity supplier.

Even if you only create one-quarter of your own power, you can significantly reduce your remaining monthly electricity costs by also opting into your utility company's off-peak power program. Most off-peak electricity programs provide you with an overall lower kWh rate, provided you significantly reduce power use on weekdays during their high-peak hours. In most circumstances, overall electrical use peaks from 11:00 AM through 6:00 PM.

Unlike most off-peak customers, however, your renewable power system will provide additional energy to your home during off-peak hours, ensuring you generally won't have issues with heating water, doing laundry, or cooling your home during off-peak periods. This benefit alone could make it practical enough to finance the installation of a renewable power system.

Resources:

[1] Nanosolar: http://www.nanosolar.com

[2] Solar Power Sizing Calculator: http://www.energyefficientchoices.com/resources/solar-power-sizing-calculator.html

[3] Wind Energy Sizing Calculator: http://www.energyefficientchoices.com/resources/wind-power-system-sizing-calculator.html

[4] Skystream 3.7 by Southwest Windpower: http://www.energyefficientchoices.com/products/skystream-wind-generator.html

[5] Net Metering Policies + Green Power Markets: http://www.eere.energy.gov/greenpower/markets/netmetering.shtml

5

Powering Your Vehicle Domestically

The final and ultimate method of taking control of your energy use is to say good-bye to the gas pumps and say hello to using electric and/or U.S.-supplied fuels to power your vehicle.

As with any new innovation, these vehicles can be expensive, but prices are dropping, and their demand has risen significantly since our demand for oil has dramatically increased fuel costs.

Although many newer car technologies have been available for quite some time, it appears as though U.S. car manufacturers have made little or no attempt to earnestly introduce these more fuel-efficient vehicles to the marketplace.

Change is inevitable, and, as bad as the oil crisis has been, the good that has come from it is a decision to change the U.S. auto industry's gas-guzzling philosophy to one of providing better performance and more environmentally safe vehicles.

Some U.S.-based car and truck manufacturers had claimed that consumers did not want the more efficient vehicles, but studies have shown that since profits are generally smaller for more efficient vehicles, many of the U.S. auto manufacturers did little or nothing to promote energy-efficient vehicles and spent millions promoting Hummers and large SUVs.

Actual surveys indicated that most consumers did not know there were usable electric or natural gas vehicles available other than as prototypes. These same consumers indicated that they might have opted to purchase these other vehicles had they known they existed.

Electric Cars and Vehicles

Even though electric cars have been available since the late 1800s, we are only now truly beginning to see the benefits of using this form of power source.

Unlike the electric cars of old, which struggled to travel up to a range of 18 miles at 14 mph, today's electric vehicles average a travel distance of at least 100 miles at speeds of 65 to 85 mph.

A few advantages of owning an electric vehicle are:

Significantly Lower Cost per Mile

For conventional gasoline combustion automobiles, at the rate of $3 per gallon, an average vehicle that is getting 24 mpg will require that you spend $12.50 to drive 100 miles.

For the new ***Phoenix Electric SUV***, at the current electric price of 0.14 per kWh, this vehicle uses 4.9 cents of power per mile to provide an equivalent 81.6 mpg. You will only have to spend $4.90 to drive 100 miles. That is less than 40 percent of the cost of using gasoline and is equivalent to paying only $1.21 per gallon of gas. (Photo courtesy of Phoenix Motor Cars.)

Significantly Lower Maintenance Costs

There's no oil to change, no air filters to block, no valves to clean, no exhaust to replace, no catalytic converter to wear out, no water pump, no oil pump, no alternator, no fuel injector to clean, no carburetor to rebuild—need I say more?

One of the main reasons that large car makers had not gotten behind electric vehicles is that there is virtually no money for them to make later on replacement parts, since many of the things that break down and need replacement in gasoline-fired engines don't even exist in the electric car.

Lower maintenance costs are also something to keep in mind when buying your first electric car. They may cost a bit more now, since they are not yet mass produced on the scale of other cars, but any extra sales costs will be compensated in time by the lack of extensive maintenance.

You Can Access Unlimited Power

Using the Phoenix Electric SUV as an example, this vehicle takes a full charge of 35 kWh. When this vehicle is plugged into a standard 120-volt electric outlet, it takes approximately six hours to recharge the batteries.

Electric vehicles could also be recharged in under fifteen minutes using an optional high-power 250 kW charger. These high-power chargers can be installed in your garage and are the same types of chargers used nationwide wherever there is an electric refueling station. High-power chargers do not use more electricity when compared to performing an overnight charge, since they use a high amount of power for a significantly shorter period of time to accomplish the same result.

If you participate with your electric utility's off-peak rate program and you recharge your vehicle overnight, you'll experience even lower operating costs for your vehicle, and your comparable cost per gallon could easily fall below one dollar.

For sources of electric fuel stations, or any alternative fuel, please view this ***Alternative Fuel Finder***[2].

Due to electricity deregulation, you get to choose your power source. If you choose wind or solar as your provider, or install your own solar or wind turbines, your car will run on a totally renewable and unlimited power source and have an absolute zero percent carbon footprint.

The benefits of driving an electric vehicle will generally outweigh any changes we may need to make to our driving habits due to their current limited driving range. With the exception of long trips, the average person drives twenty-five to forty miles to and from work each day, which still falls within this car's one-hundred-mile range. This limitation will soon be old news, since improvements in battery technology may extend the electric car's driving range up to two hundred fifty miles.

Hybrid Cars and Vehicles

For drivers who want to be green, but who travel many miles a day, hybrid cars are a great alternative, since they use both gasoline and electricity to provide less emissions and improved driving range.

There are a variety of methods car manufacturers use to create their hybrid version of a car, but the basic premise is that both a small gasoline engine and a high-torque electric motor are used to provide a combination of acceleration power and driving power that uses current technology in a very efficient manner.

Today's hybrids, however, are only a shadow of things to come. Most current hybrids utilize a small percentage of electric power and use the gas-driven engine to create this electricity in lieu of allowing you to plug it in. It's as though the car manufacturers are purposely making it difficult for you to even begin to distance yourself from having to depend upon gasoline.

Current hybrids also employ a typical method of using the electric motor to provide initial acceleration; then, the electric motor cuts out at about 25 to 30 mph and the gasoline engine takes over from there. This results in a smaller gasoline engine being sufficient, and it decreases fuel consumption.

If you do a lot of city driving, a hybrid vehicle will provide a great advantage, since it uses the electric motor to initiate all the constant accelerations, but if you primarily drive on the highway, the savings are almost insignificant when compared to how much more you will pay for the vehicle.

I am still waiting for the true hybrid to appear which provides both a self-chargeable electric system that will take you up to one hundred miles, plus a fuel-based engine that will be there to provide extended driving distances when necessary. The closest possible runner-up would be the Chevy Volt, which is not set for release until 2010.

Of course, when it comes to hybrids and our desire to eliminate our use of foreign fuels, the best combination would be a vehicle that uses an electric system along with a biodiesel, ethanol, or natural gas fuel source. I know this, now you know this, and I think the automotive industry finally admits they know this. Now we'll just have to wait and see what they do with this information.

Natural Gas Cars

At this time, the Honda Civic GX, which uses *compressed natural gas* (CNG), is the only production natural gas vehicle (NGV) available in the United States. The U.S. Environmental Protection Agency has dubbed this vehicle as "The cleanest internal combustion vehicle on Earth."

NGVs are much cleaner than gasoline or diesel vehicles, as indicated by these statistics:

- Carbon monoxide emissions are reduced 90 to 97 percent.

- Carbon dioxide emissions are reduced 25 percent.

- Nitrogen oxide emissions are reduced 35 to 60 percent.

- Toxic and carcinogenic pollutant emissions are greatly reduced.

CNG is currently available from over 1,500 locations throughout the United States. The U.S. Department of Energy provides a current listing of ***Natural Gas Refilling Stations***[3]. In addition, natural gas fuel can also be obtained from your own filling machine if natural gas is available in your home.

Since the United States has a vast supply of natural gas available domestically, this fuel source will help us to dramatically reduce our dependency on foreign fuels, while we continue to work toward developing new technologies that will eventually eliminate the need of combustion fuels in vehicles.

More perks:

- Natural Gas Vehicle fuel storage tanks are thicker and stronger than gasoline tanks.

- On average, natural gas costs one-third less than gasoline.

- An existing natural gas distribution system already exists within the United States to deliver natural gas to almost every city and many suburban areas.

- In the past, natural gas prices have proven to be quite stable when compared to the prices of petroleum-based fuels.

Recently, through the introduction of the ***Pickens Plan***[4], the push for backing natural gas vehicles has really taken off. Although natural gas vehicles are not seen as an answer to global warming, they can help reduce our demand on foreign fuels long enough to allow us to create some truly energy-efficient vehicles that run on water and electricity.

Hydrogen Fuel Cell Vehicles

Fuel cells can be used to produce electricity to drive electric vehicles in lieu of gasoline engines. In a fuel cell vehicle, hydrogen is used to activate the fuel cell and create electricity. This electricity then charges batteries, which in turn power an electric motor that propels the vehicle. Water is the only by-product left behind.

There is no existing hydrogen distribution system within the United States, so it first appears as though hydrogen would not be a fuel source to consider; however, natural gas, which already has a distribution system, can be used to create hydrogen.

Hydrogen can also be produced through electrolysis, which is a process that uses electricity to split water into hydrogen and oxygen. Using this system, huge wind turbines could be installed in the ocean and use their electricity to separate the hydrogen and oxygen molecules from the water. The oxygen would be released into the air, reducing the effects of deforestation, and the hydrogen would be collected to fuel our vehicles.

Honda again appears to be the front-runner in providing vehicles using the latest energy efficiency technologies, as it introduced its FCX Clarity hydrogen fuel cell vehicle. This vehicle gets a range of 620 kilometers, or 385 miles, finally answering the question of why hydrogen-powered electric cars can perform better than cars that rely solely upon stored battery energy for power.

For sources of hydrogen, or any alternative fuel, please view this ***Alternative Fuel Finder***[2].

....

Resources:

[1] Phoenix Electric SUV: http://www.phoenixmotorcars.com/

2 Alternative Fuel Finder: http://www.eere.energy.gov/afdc/stations/find_station.php

3 Natural Gas Refilling Stations: http://www.eere.energy.gov/afdc/fuels/natural_gas_locations.html

4 Pickens Plan: http://www.energyefficientchoices.com/pickens-plan/

6

Funding and Loan Sources

Many of my energy-conservation ideas can be performed gradually on your existing budget. If you are looking to perform any major upgrades, such as insulating your home, replacing your windows and doors, installing a solar water heating system, or installing a renewable energy system using wind or solar power, it may be necessary to borrow money today so that you can reap the benefits for all the years to come.

Energy Mortgages

With such a dramatic increase in building energy-efficient homes or making energy-efficiency improvements to existing homes, mortgage lenders who want to ensure they acquire the business of energy-minded consumers are taking advantage of the current trend by offering Energy Efficient Mortgages (EEM) on new homes or Energy Improvement Mortgages (EIM) on existing homes.

An energy mortgage increases your capacity to obtain a higher loan by allowing mortgage lenders to include the energy savings of proposed improvements to qualify as additional income. Likewise, a lending institution may opt to simply see that you could afford a higher mortgage that includes the cost of energy improvements, based upon resulting lower monthly energy expenses.

To apply for an energy mortgage, you must first have the property inspected by an energy-efficiency professional who will provide the home with an energy rating. This information is necessary for your lender to see whether the home qualifies for an energy mortgage.

By including your energy-efficient project costs into your mortgage, you should find that any increase in your loan payments are very close to the amount of energy costs being saved on average through the year. Of course, as years pass and utility costs increase, your savings will also increase, as you will not be as affected by utility cost increases.

Energy-efficient based mortgage programs, available through Fannie Mae, FHA, and the VA, have taken on new underwriting guidelines to ensure that financing energy-efficient homes is easier for the consumer.

FHA-Insured Loans. For new homes, the FHA will allow a loan addition of 5 percent of the home's assessed value, starting at $4,000, to a maximum of $8,000 per loan. For more in-depth information, visit the ***HUD Web site***[1].

VA-Insured Loans. For new homes, the VA will allow a loan increase up to $3,000 based upon documented costs only, while they will extend the loans limit to $6,000 if the projected home energy rating will result in a reduction of energy costs that exceeds the increase of the mortgage cost. For more in-depth information, visit the ***VA Web site***[2].

Fannie Mae-Insured Loans. For new homes, Fannie Mae will allow a loan increase up to 5 percent of the home's assessed value. For existing home retrofits, Fannie Mae will allow a loan increase up to 15 percent. For more in-depth information, visit the ***Fannie Mae Web site***[3].

Tax Breaks, Tax Credits, and Incentives

There has been some form of energy-related tax breaks or tax credits available since the energy crisis in the 70s; however, these incentives had thinned out quite a lot until recent years.

Since the types and levels of tax breaks or tax credits can vary greatly from one year to the next, I almost chose not to list this information, since it may be out of date within a year or two of this publication. To overcome this issue, I have chosen simply to state that some form of government tax break or tax credit is likely to be in effect for decades to come. The samples of current tax breaks and tax credits I publish are simply to serve as a guide for what types of breaks are currently available and may still be available in the future.

As with all tax-related issues, before making any major purchase where you may depend upon a tax break or tax credit, I suggest you first confirm the specific details of current tax laws with an accountant or financial adviser.

The Clean Energy Tax Stimulus Act of 2008

At this time, The Clean Energy Tax Stimulus Act of 2008 provides several incentives for residential homeowners and commercial business owners to invest in conservation related improvements and renewable energy installations.

The energy act extends dates for many existing programs that were due to expire prior to the year 2008. Although a lot of material is covered in the Clean Energy Tax Stimulus Act of 2008, I was able to focus in on two primary updates that specifically help residential homeowners.

Section 103 indicates how taxpayers can claim a personal tax credit equal to 30 percent of qualifying expenditures, with a maximum $2,000 credit, for the purchase of property that uses solar energy to generate electricity for use in a dwelling unit and also for a qualified solar water-heating property. This does not apply to instances where the primary purpose is to heat swimming pools or hot tubs.

Section 201 provides a 10 percent investment tax credit for energy-efficiency improvements to existing homes with respect to advanced main-air circulating fans, furnaces using natural gas, propane, or oil, and also for improvements associated with hot water boilers, windows and doors, and some forms of pellet stoves.

State Level Incentives

Many state and local governments, as well as local and regional utility companies, also provide incentives for you to become more energy efficient. In many cases, you could reduce your overall energy improvement costs by 25 percent or more by taking the time to find all the sources of funding available.

Since it could be a daunting task to track down the agencies, authorities, and government officials that might be of help to you, a comprehensive collection of information on state, local, and utility incentives that promote renewable energy and energy efficiency is provided by ***DSIRE (Database of State Incentives for Renewables and Efficiency)***[4]

Financing Sample

Depending upon where you live, your out-of-pocket expense for the installation of a solar power system can vary greatly. The following is just a sample of what may be available to you when you are looking to perform large energy-efficiency improvements in your home.

For our sample, I have set a base where the customer is fully dependent upon electricity for his heating, air conditioning, water heating, and cooking needs and typically uses 2,300 kWh of power per month. The system will be designed to provide for 60 percent of his total electric needs and has a lifetime expectancy of twenty-five years.

The focus is to locate where funding can be obtained and to see if the monthly impact on expenses could be justified. Always bear in mind that any extra monthly expense, provided it is affordable, will eventually lead to a significant reduction in overall monthly expenses once the financing has been paid in full.

For example, installing this solar power system in Arizona would require a solar system size of 9 kW, which would utilize approximately 900 square feet of roof or land. The average expected installation cost would be $81,000.

The total cost would be reduced by applying a state and federal tax credit of $3,000 and also by applying a rebate from the utility company of $27,000 (based upon providing $3 per watt of system size: 9,000 watts x $3 = $27,000). These incentives reduce the overall cost of the project to $51,000.

Having sized the solar system to provide for 60 percent of the home's electrical needs, you could expect to save $150 per month during the first year. With an average increase of electric utility costs at 3.5 percent per year, you could expect to save an average of $211 per month after ten years, $297 per month after twenty years, and up to $353 per month after twenty-five years. When looking at the twenty-five-year expected lifetime of this solar power system, you could expect an average savings of $251 per month, for a total of $75,300 in savings overall.

If you had the capacity to pay the $51,000 for the installation without having to borrow, your payback period would be approximately seventeen years. Since you would have spent this money anyway on electricity bills, it actually cost you nothing to install the system. The great benefit is that the $24,000 in savings over the next eight years or more is like pure profit that cost you nothing to achieve, while being very helpful to the environment at the same time.

Alternatively, if you need to borrow this money, let's look at the expected loan costs by taking advantage of a low-interest Energy-Efficient Mortgage, when a loan rate of 4.5 percent is secured.

A twenty-year term loan on $51,000 would require a monthly payment of $322.65, with total payments equaling $ 77,436. Since $26,436 of this amount would be interest, using an average tax rate of 30 percent, you would realize tax savings of approximately $7,900 during the term of the loan, reducing your true costs to $69,536. This lower total results in a payback period of approximately twenty-three years. Since your monthly payments would exceed what your actual utility costs would have been, you will have paid off the system three years early and will experience an approximate savings of $15,000 over the remaining five or more years of system life.

The overall concept is that the money you save on electrical utility bills will offset the money it would cost to install a renewable power system. In addition, the system may provide several additional years of service after it has been paid off, resulting in substantial savings overall.

Behind the scenes is one more benefit that is often overlooked. The renewable power system has added value to your home, and you can get 80 percent of this returned to you if you sell your home. There is no losing when it comes to installing a renewable power system for your home.

Resources:

1 HUD Web site: http://www.hud.gov
2 VA Web site: http://www.va.gov/
3 Fannie Mae Web site: http://www.fanniemae.com/
4 DSIRE (Database of State Incentives for Renewables and Efficiency): http://www.dsireusa.org/

7

Our Energy-Efficiency Synopsis

So, what does it all mean? How can you truly be energy efficient and yet select affordable methods to do so? The previous chapters answered this, but they also provided a lot of information, and so we designed this chapter to act as a recap or a quick reference for future use.

Stop Wasting Energy in Your Home

For a moment, forget those cool-looking solar panel systems and forget about having a graceful wind turbine in your yard. Back up for a moment to take in the bigger picture and see that the first, easiest, and least expensive way to cut energy costs and save money is to stop wasting what is already being used on a daily basis.

By cutting out the waste, you will get a significant return on any expense—plus, if you eventually did want to install solar or wind power, you would be able to go with a smaller system and still save some money.

The most economical ways to reduce the amount of energy you waste in your home are:

- Add more insulation to your walls and attic space.

- Seal your home to reduce or eliminate air infiltration.

- Replace existing incandescent bulbs with energy-saving compact fluorescent lamps (CFLs) or LED bulbs.

- Replace existing appliances (refrigerators, dishwashers, washing machines, dryers) with Energy Star-rated appliances.

- Use smart energy strips to eliminate wasted computer power.

Upgrade or Replace Your Heating and Cooling Systems

If you have not already done so, eliminate any fossil fuel as the prime heating source in your home. The idea is to use some form of electricity to provide for your primary heating needs, since electricity is the only energy source that can be generated at very high efficiencies and can also be created by yourself at some future date.

The best choice for heating your home is with a high-efficiency heat pump system that uses electricity to gather heat that is freely available in the outdoor air or in the ground.

The primary advantages of using a heat pump are:

- Significantly reduced heating costs compared to most fossil fuels and electric resistance heat.

- There is an unlimited source of heat potential in the ground and air.

- It is much healthier than using fossil fuels and there is no need of carbon monoxide detectors in the home.

- Heat is not wasted as it is with most fossil fuels, which require exhaust vents of some form.

Replace Your Water Heating System

Next to your home heating and cooling system, your water heating system is the item in your home that likely consumes the greatest amount of power. On average, water heating consumes 25 percent of home energy use.

There are a few very efficient methods of turning the tide on home hot water creation:

Heat Pump Water Heaters. These heaters work just like heat pumps for your home heating, in that they use electricity to gather heat that is freely available in the air. Depending upon the climate, the amount of heat generated by the heat pump may fully heat your water or may only partially heat your water, and then electric heaters would conclude heating the water to the required temperature. These systems can easily reduce your energy costs by 25 percent or more.

Tankless Electric Water Heaters. These heaters use extreme amounts of power to instantaneously heat your water to the preset temperature. They use power only for the time that the hot water is being used, and then they turn completely off and use no energy at all to preheat or store hot water. These systems can easily reduce your hot water heating costs by 40 percent.

Solar Water Heaters. These water heaters take full advantage of the energy freely provided by the sun and create hot water via exposed dark piping that directly heats or preheats your hot water. As with the heat pump water heater in northern climates, you may want to use this as a preheater with an existing hot water system. In warm climates this system can provide 60 percent or more of your hot water at no additional cost beyond installation.

Create Your Own Power with Solar Panels and Wind Turbines

For those who have good levels of sun or consistent wind throughout the year, the only issues with using solar or wind energy to help power their homes are the initial cost and the availability of space.

Prices on new solar and wind technologies are coming down and will eventually become affordable for anyone. Even if you only have the capacity to offset 25 percent of your own power needs, this still means that for every four homes that do this, one entire home is virtually off the grid.

Solar Power Systems

Common panel types are monocrystalline, polycrystalline, and amorphous, which vary slightly with output capacities and their capacities to generate power from direct sunlight versus low light conditions.

Since geographic location matters when selecting a solar system, it is advisable to first use this ***Solar Power Sizing Calculator***[1].

Once you have an idea of the capacity of the system you can afford, you'll want to confirm that you have good southern exposure on your roof or an area of unobstructed land on your property.

Wind Turbine Systems

Wind power has been harnessed for centuries by farmers to crush grain or pump water, and now it's available to almost anyone who wants to generate free power.

Two types of wind turbines are available. Horizontal Axis Wind Turbines (HAWT) are the typical forms you have seen where a set of blades rotates in the wind. These are the most common form of turbines, but they do require an acre or two of unobstructed wind to perform at their best.

Vertical Axis Wind Turbines (VAWT) are relatively new and look more like a hamster wheel turned sideways. Their primary advantage is that they work well within close proximity of trees and structures and may be more adaptable to the average home where land space is minimal.

To see a close estimate of what the available wind energy is for your geographic area, use this ***Wind Energy Sizing Calculator***[2].

Power Distribution

Most utility companies now offer net metering. This means that for any renewable power system you install, you will stay connected to the grid and can sell your excess power back to the utility company.

You can access the ***Net Metering Policies***[3] of most utility companies at the U.S. Department of Energy's Web site to verify whether your electrical utility company offers net metering.

When connecting your renewable power system to the grid with net metering, you may still experience power outages if your electrical utility company loses power for any reason. If this were to happen while your renewable power system is generating power, your system might provide some power to your home; however, you should not expect your renewable power system to behave like a backup power system. A backup power system is designed to provide for most or all of your power needs, but most renewable power systems are only designed to provide for a fraction of your power needs.

Since most solar or wind systems only generate a fraction of what the home truly consumes, a net metering system provides you with temporary power credit when you use less power than you create and returns this credit to you when you use more power than you create.

For example, your solar panels may output a lot of power while you are not at home, thus running your meter backward, but later that day when you return and use more power than your solar panels can handle, your meter resumes turning clockwise, and you burn off the credit.

The net metering system allows you to forgo the costs and maintenance issues associated with maintaining a battery system. Without net metering, your renewable energy system could not connect to the grid, and you would need a battery system to store unused power.

Regardless of the costs, you will eventually get your money back. The time span for payback will vary with your geographic location, since sun exposure and wind currents vary across the United States, but no matter how you slice it, you will have reduced your carbon footprint on this planet, and you can't put a price on that.

Drive Away from Foreign Fuels

As much as energy efficiency has been a topic for over a decade, it was not until gas prices began rising so sharply that America truly decided to once again jump on the fuel-efficiency bandwagon.

What will work best for you will depend upon your specific needs and even your geographic location, so take a look now at this selection of alternative-vehicle options.

The Electric Car

Electric cars operate at less than one-third the cost of gasoline engines and require significantly less maintenance as well. Overall, an electric car is the perfect vehicle—except for the final hitch that has held it back: its limited driving range.

Today's electric cars can travel about one hundred miles before recharging. If charging stations are available in your area, this is fine, since the vehicle can be recharged in about fifteen minutes with the use of a high-power charger. If you live in those areas without charging stations, you cannot make any plans to drive more than forty miles away from home.

Technology, however, does not stand still. New batteries that will be available shortly will increase driving range to two hundred fifty miles, ensuring a more prominent place for the electric car in our society.

The greenest choice you could make is to install several solar panels for the sole purpose of powering your car's power charger. In effect, you would drive totally green and have a zero percent carbon footprint.

The Hybrid Car

Hybrid vehicles are basically standard combustion-engine vehicles that have been downsized slightly, since they use electric motors to accelerate the car to about 25 mph before the combustion engine starts.

This form of locomotion really improves gas mileage in the city, where there are many reasons to continuously accelerate, but this offers little or no extra efficiency for highway driving.

Other hybrids are on the drawing boards that offer better efficiency by allowing you to drive the first one hundred miles or so on pure battery power before the combustion engine takes over. This is more practical and will attract more drivers than the hybrids being offered today.

The Natural Gas Car

Natural gas vehicles (NGVs) still burn a combustible fuel, but, when compared to gasoline engines, their carbon monoxide emissions are 90 to 97 percent less, their carbon dioxide emissions are 25 percent less and their nitrogen oxide emissions are 35 to 60 percent less.

Natural gas vehicles also cost less to drive per gallon compared to current gas prices. Even though there may be no specific natural gas refilling stations in place, natural gas is widely distributed throughout the entire U.S. and can easily be made available locally and may already be available in your home.

It is the hope of many that we embrace natural gas vehicles in order to curb our use of foreign oil and buy ourselves a decade or so to put even better forms of electric vehicles in place.

The Hydrogen Fuel Cell Car

The hydrogen fuel cell car is simply an electric car that uses hydrogen to create the electricity it needs to run the motor.

This form of transportation is a few years away from being both available and affordable, but it provides the opportunity for a fully electric car to exceed the one-hundred-mile traveling limitation. This alone could lead our society to truly embrace this form of transportation.

In a Nutshell

You can start by doing everything you can to steer away from foreign fossil fuels—by using U.S.-supplied resources, while also working to establish your own energy independence by making full use of solar, wind, water, and fuel cell technology.

You can play a pivotal role during the next twenty years as this nation heads toward making a historic change in the way we define energy sources. Each person's decision to choose energy sources that are forever renewable and pollution free will reinforce the same decision made by millions of others who also want our fossil fuel dependency to end.

When we all unite under the same cause to become a nation that embraces the use of renewable energy sources, our bonds to fossil fuels will finally be broken, and we will live a life of energy independence.

Resources:

1 Solar Power Sizing Calculator: http://www.energyefficientchoices.com/resources/solar-power-sizing-calculator.html

2 Wind Energy Sizing Calculator: http://www.energyefficientchoices.com/resources/wind-power-system-sizing-calculator.html

3 Net Metering Policies: http://www.eere.energy.gov/greenpower/markets/netmetering.shtml

About The Author

David Nelmes is a Home Energy Inspector in Pennsylvania, specializing in the fields of Heating and Air Conditioning, Electrical Wiring, and Interiors/Insulation.

David's career highlights include the position of assistant electrical construction engineer for three nuclear power plants; serving as an administrator, engineer, and installer in the heating and air conditioning field; and working as primary Webmaster, administrator, and advertising consultant for a well-established home and garden Web site business.

David lives in Northeast Pennsylvania with his wonderful and supportive wife, Karlene, and spends his time writing, performing home energy audits, and developing Web sites.

Glossary of Terms

AC Voltage. AC stands for Alternating Current, which is set at 60 Hz (hertz) or 60 cycles per second in the United States. AC voltage used in homes is generally between 110 and 120 volts. The advantage of AC is that it can be sent long distances with little loss of overall power and can be easily stepped up to higher voltages or dropped down to lower voltages with the use of a transformer.

Air Source Heat Pumps. See *Heat Pump.* An air source heat pump extracts its heat from outside air by forcing that air to pass over finely finned coils in the outdoor condensing unit. This style of heat pump can typically function well even at temperatures just below freezing. Cold-climate heat pumps provide even greater performance at lower temperatures.

BTU. BTU stands for British Thermal Unit, which is the amount of energy necessary to increase the temperature of one pound of water one degree. This term is generally used in conjunction with heating and air conditioning systems.

Carbon Footprint. The average carbon footprint for a U.S. household is fifteen to twenty metric tons of carbon dioxide (CO_2) per year. This indicates the level of carbon you create by living here on earth while using its resources. The more fossil fuels you burn, the greater your carbon footprint. The more products you consume from manufacturers who do not take the environment into consideration, the greater your carbon footprint.

Compact Fluorescent Lamps. CFLs: Compact fluorescent lamps create light by exciting a gas trapped within a glass chamber. These new compact versions are generally provided with a swirl shape and have been adapted to fit standard light sockets that were originally used exclusively for incandescent bulbs. CFLs use much less electricity to create the amount of light we were accustomed to with standard incandescent light bulbs. For example, a 13-watt CFL creates an equivalent 60 watts of light, and a 20-watt CFL creates an equivalent

75 watts of light. On average, CFLs use about 75 percent less power than incandescent bulbs.

Company Homes. During many early mining booms, or with a sudden industrialization of an area, owners of the businesses often built homes or entire villages to attract workers. These homes were generally built to minimal standards and did not include any heat or cold-retaining values. At the time this was somewhat normal, but as time passed, and these homes aged, their appearance was often enhanced, but their overall insulating value was often not improved, and they serve as the least efficient homes still available at this time.

Compressed Natural Gas. CNG: This is no different than the natural gas you may use for heating your home, but it is under a much higher pressure, about 3,000 to 4,000 PSI, so that it takes up less room. Cars that use CNG have specially designed tanks to handle this high pressure safely.

CFLs. See Compact Fluorescent Lamps

Chimney Effect. Any tall hollow space that has an opening near the bottom and at the top will develop a natural flow of air that pulls air in the bottom and out the top, provided the air temperature at the bottom is warmer than the outside air temperature. This is caused by the warm air in the pipe that wants to rise. As it rises, it creates a vacuum behind itself which results in more air being pulled in from below.

CNG. See Compressed Natural Gas

Coefficient Of Performance. COP: This is the degree to which a rated heat pump uses electricity to generate heat. If a heat pump can create 14 kW of heat when using only 4 kW of power, it would have a COP of 3.5, since it created 3 1/2 times the heat that electricity alone would have provided. In easier terms, you pay for 4 kW to run the heat pump, and you get 14 kW to heat your home. That means you get 14 - 4 = 10 kW from the air or earth, depending upon your heat pump style. Those kilowatts are free—you did not have to pay for them.

COP. See Coefficient of Performance

CRT Monitors. CRT stands for Cathode Ray Tube, which is simply the standard television tube we are familiar with. CRT monitors are used with computer systems. They started out very small, only twelve inches at first, with only amber or green text colors, and they eventually grew up to twenty-one inches or larger with over 16.7 million colors. Their popularity is currently falling, as they are being replaced by LCD flat screen displays.

DC Voltage. DC stands for Direct Current and is what you would normally associate with the type of power provided by batteries. Renewable energy items, such as solar panels, create 12 volts DC (12 VDC) to 24 volts DC (24 VDC). If you are using this system to charge batteries, the DC power could be used as is, but if the intention is to power household items, you would first need to feed the DC power into a power inverter that transforms the DC power into AC power.

Dehumidify. To remove humidity from the air. Basements and garages are often prone to having increased humidity levels, since moisture tends to enter those areas through concrete walls and floors. A comfortable humidity level in the home is approximately 35 to 40 percent. When humidity levels exceed 55 percent, the possibility for mold growth exists, especially for darker and less ventilated areas such as basements.

Electrical Resistance Heat. This type of heat is provided through the standard electric heating element found on electric stoves, in electric ovens, in electric water heaters, and in electric baseboard heaters. This form of heat is 99.9% efficient.

Energy Conservation. The act of not using more energy than necessary to perform a function is energy conservation. For example, if you want 100 watts of light in a room, you could use a 100-watt incandescent bulb or a 23-watt CFL. The CFL provides the same result at nearly one-quarter of the power requirement. Likewise, a non-insulated wall in your home may allow 200 BTUHs of heat to pass through to the outside, while the same wall with R-13 insulation would decrease that amount to 25 BTUHs.

Energy Efficient. When any given item uses less power or resources than an older existing item, it is considered more efficient than what is currently being used and is therefore energy efficient.

Energy Efficient Strategies. Plans and ideas wherein the overall goal is to reduce wasted energy, such as recycling, pursuing renewable energy options, remodeling your home to better retain its desired temperature, etc.

Energy Independence. This is the result of being able to safely rely upon renewable energy sources such as solar, wind, and water. Nonrenewable energy sources, such as oil, gas, and coal, whether they are foreign or domestic, create a form of bondage in that their existence fades with each use. Anything that gradually runs out and also destroys your environment as you use it can only create fear while we are using it and fear of how to survive once it's gone. That's energy bondage.

Energy Saving Smart Strip. A specially designed power strip that provides an easier method of saving power by automatically shutting down equipment we often leave running. This smart strip works great with computer systems and home entertainment systems.

Foreign Fuel. Any form of fossil fuel that is obtained through drilling or mining in a country other than the country you live in.

Energy Vampires. Devices and equipment that consume power, even when you are not using them, such as cell phone chargers, clocks on coffee pots, VCR and DVD players, televisions, computers, monitors and displays, printers, answering machines, stereos, etc.

Fossil Fuel. Any fuel source that was created by the process of ancient plant life having been buried for millions of years until they became hard as coal, or fluid as oil, or as clear and light as natural gas.

Fuel Cells. In a fuel cell, using hydrogen and oxygen as its fuel source, an electrochemical reaction takes place between the hydrogen and oxygen that directly converts chemical energy into electrical energy. The short version is that hydrogen is used to activate the fuel cell and create electricity. In a fuel cell car, this electricity powers the vehicle's electric motor. Water and heat are the only by-products of a hydrogen fuel cell.

Geothermal Heat Pumps. See Heat Pump: A geothermal heat pump extracts its heat from either the ground or groundwater. For either heating or cooling purposes, a geothermal heat pump has a consistent ground temperature to work with that rarely drops below 45 degrees F or 20 degrees C. This allows it to provide a steady COP (coefficient of performance) of around 3.5 to 4.

Global Warming. Many scientists have claimed that the temperature of the earth is gradually rising due to the effects of mankind having released billions of tons of carbon dioxide into the atmosphere. We have done this in just moments of time, compared to how long it took to store that energy in the earth in the first place. Carbon dioxide is a greenhouse gas, which holds heat very well, with the result that the earth's temperature is warming too quickly.

Grid-Tie. This term is normally associated with electric utility companies that provide net metering and allow you to tie your solar or wind turbine power into their power lines and distribution system. This allows you to send your excess power out, while also allowing you to draw in power as you need it.

HAWT. See Horizontal Axis Wind Turbine

Heat Pump. A heat pump is an electrically powered device that gathers and moves heat. When you use a heat pump in the summer, it gathers heat from inside your home and exhausts it outside. When you use a heat pump in the winter, it gathers heat from the outside air or from below the ground and exhausts that heat into your home. When heating, heat pumps generally have 2 to 3 times the capacity to provide heat than electricity alone could have provided.

Horizontal Axis Wind Turbine. HAWT: The horizontal-style wind turbine generally has three or four blades that spin on a horizontally positioned shaft. This type of blade system works best when positioned thirty feet or more high in the air, and at least one hundred to two hundred feet horizontally away from any turbulent air caused by nearby trees or homes. Typical residential scale sizes range from providing 500 watts to 10 kilowatts.

HSPF. Heating Seasonal Performance Factor: This is the most commonly used measure of the heating efficiency of heat pumps. The HSPF is a heat pump's approximate seasonal heating output in BTUs divided by the amount of energy in watt-hours it consumes. This is a seasonal measure, which takes into consideration the fact that heat pumps run for different percentages of the day during the spring and fall.

Hybrid Car. This is a vehicle that uses more than one energy source to provide locomotion. Currently this type of vehicle uses an electric motor to initiate the vehicle's acceleration and then engages the combustion engine upon reaching 25 mph, thereby allowing for a smaller-sized combustion engine, which conserves fuel use even further.

Incandescent Bulbs. These are the standard type of light bulbs we have all grown up with. They use a tungsten coil between two electric probes. When we apply power, this coil gets super hot and glows, providing light. The problem with this form of light is that more energy is transformed into heat than into light.

Infiltration. The process of air seeping into a space. In our homes, this is generally an unwanted event. Air that infiltrates through poor window and door seals, cracks along the home's foundation, or any nondesigned source for air entry, can increase heating and cooling costs and create the sensation of drafts during the winter.

Kill-A-Watt Meter. This is a very handy device that aids you in determining the power that any 110/120-volt device or piece of equipment may be using. This can help you determine whether an appliance is in need of repair and also can help motivate you to use more efficient devices.

kWh. Kilowatt-hour: The amount of watts used in an hour times 1,000 (kilo). Electrical utility companies charge by the kilowatt-hour. If your utility rate was 14 cents per kilowatt-hour, and if you used fifteen hundred kilowatts in any given month, your bill could be 1500 kWh x $0.12 = $180, plus taxes, fees, etc.

LCD Flat Screen Displays. This is the most current version of display used for computer monitors and television viewing. Instead of using a massive cathode ray tube (CRT) and huge amounts of power to energize that tube, LCD flat panel displays simply power each pixel individually with the end result being a sharper picture, smaller enclosure, much less heat, and significantly less power consumed.

LED Bulb. Light Emitting Diode: These bulbs consist of clusters of white or clear LEDs that are arranged to emit their light outward. These lights use about half the power of standard CFLs, but unlike CFLs, LED bulbs can be dimmed and have a significantly longer life cycle, in the order of 70,000 hours. Unlike CFLs, they contain no mercury and do not make an environmental impact when disposed of—if they ever burn out.

Natural Gas Vehicle. These vehicles are extremely clean-burning internal combustion vehicles. When compared to gasoline-driven vehicles, NGVs' carbon monoxide emissions are reduced 90 to 97 percent, their carbon dioxide emissions are reduced 25 percent, their nitrogen oxide emissions are reduced 35 to 60 percent and their toxic and carcinogenic pollutant emissions are greatly reduced. They are also the choice vehicle for the next decade or two via the Pickens Plan.

NGV. See Natural Gas Vehicle

Net Metering. In conjunction with a solar power system or wind power generation system, this is an interface agreement whereby your electrical utility company provides the means that allows you to sell them your unused electricity or provide you with credit that you may use in the future at no cost. Variations may exist with each utility company as to how they credit the power you provide.

Off-Grid. This is normally associated with solar or wind power systems. When you are off-grid, you have no connection to any electric utility distribution system. This requires that the power you generate is stored in an array of batteries and is generally then transformed into AC power for general appliance and electronics use.

Photovoltaic. A technology where solar cells collect solar energy from the sun and convert this power into electricity.

Power Inverter. A device used in solar and wind power systems to convert DC current into AC current that can be used within the home (and within the utility company's electrical distribution system provided net metering is available).

Power Vampires. See Energy Vampire

PV. See Photovoltaic

Recovery Rates. Recovery rates are determined by the number of gallons in an hour that a water heater can reheat to its designated temperature. Standard electric water heaters have a recovery rate of about twenty gallons per hour. Gas water heaters have a recovery rate of about thirty-five gallons per hour. Both electric or gas tankless water heaters provide unlimited hot water, so a recovery rate does not apply.

Renewable Energy. Any form of energy that is provided through a source that has almost endless supply, such as solar, wind, hydroelectric, tidal generators, and even switchgrass-based ethanol.

Ridge Vent. A ridge vent is a three- to four-inch opening cut along a long portion of a roof's peak. This opening is then capped off with an enclosure that includes a screen to keep out insects and a hood to keep out rain and snow. This vent allows air to much more easily circulate within the attic space, reducing any problems with condensation and also reducing the buildup of heat during summer months.

R-Value. This is a value that is assigned to material with respect to how easily heat can pass though it. The easier it is for heat to pass through, the lower the R or Resistance-to-heat value. Likewise, the harder it is for heat to pass through, the higher the R or Resistance-to-heat value. R-13 is a typical value of wall insulation for a wall cavity size of three and a half inches.

Seasonal Energy Efficiency Rating. SEER: This is used to measure the efficiency of residential central air conditioning systems over their entire seasonal use and can be calculated by dividing the seasonal BTU of cooling by the seasonal watt-hours used. As of January, 2006, the minimum allowable SEER rating is 13. A higher SEER reflects a more efficient cooling system.

SEER. See Seasonal Energy Efficiency Rating

Solar Energy Systems. By combining multiple solar panels together, with the average panel providing 180 watts, you can create a potential level of power to provide for 25 percent or more of your home's power needs. Solar panels generate DC power, so this power is either sent directly to a power inverter or to a battery system and then to a power inverter. The power inverter transforms the DC power into the AC power your home can easily use.

Solar Panels. Generally comprised of monocrystalline or polycrystalline material which is sensitive to sunlight. As sunlight hits these panels, a reaction occurs that causes the flow of electrons. By placing these cells in the desired series and parallel arrays, you can obtain the desired voltage and amperage. To date, the average solar panel is less than 15 percent efficient.

Solar Powered Exhaust Vents. These vents are installed either on the roof or at the roof ends as gable vents. They use only the power of the sun to provide this extra ventilation and can generally be set to run at all times or just at attic temperatures of 90 degrees or higher. Since there is no wiring necessary, any basic carpenter or handyman can install this form of vent.

Tankless Water Heaters. Electric and gas-powered devices that heat water without using the conventional method of heating and maintaining a forty- to fifty-gallon supply of hot water. Tankless water heaters use a tremendous amount of energy, for short spurts of time, only when somebody draws hot water. The overall cost to heat the water drops by 25 percent or more, since no power is wasted to store the water.

Turbulent Air. With respect to the use of wind turbines, turbulent air is the effect of normally straight horizontal air streams being shifted to varying angles and into spinning vortexes as they pass over rooftops, trees, or any other high obstruction to air flow. Horizontal-style wind turbines are very sensitive to turbulence, whereas vertical-style wind turbines actually thrive in these conditions.

UPS. Uninterruptible Power Supply: A device that is often used with computer systems to help prevent nuisance shutdowns due to power flickers or power failures. UPSes also incorporate surge protection, brownout control, and low-voltage control issues. A UPS works by charging a battery that will act as your source of power instead of power directly from the grid. This works by converting the batteries' DC power back to the AC power your computer needs. When the power goes out or fluctuates, your computer is totally unaffected, since you are not connected directly to your home's power, but to a battery that is part of the UPS system. Most UPS systems provide five minutes or more of power when a total power failure has occurred, allowing you time to save your files and shut down your computer system.

VAWT. See Vertical Axis Wind Turbine

Vertical Axis Wind Turbine. VAWT: The vertical-style wind turbine generally has from three to twenty blades that spin on a vertically positioned shaft. This type of blade system works well in normal or turbulent air conditions and therefore is not as limited by requiring large areas of unobstructed land. Some versions even sit on a home's rooftop. Typical residential scale sizes range from those providing five hundred watts to ten kilowatts.

Watt. Power: The result of multiplying any voltage level by the amount of current, or amps, being consumed. For example, a standard 60-watt bulb gets that designation, since 120 volts allows .5 amps to run through this bulb size, resulting in 120 volts x .5 amps = 60 watts.

Wind Turbine System. Such a system consists of a wind turbine, tower, and power inverter. For residential situations, both horizontal- and vertical-style turbines could be used to provide a range of from five hundred watts to ten kilowatts or more for your home's power needs. Turbines that generate DC power will require a power inverter. Some turbines, such as the Sky Stream, have a built-in power converter. The power inverter transforms DC power into the AC power your home can easily use.

Resources

Web Site References

Chapter 1

[1] Dryer Vent Seal: http://www.energyefficientchoices.com/products/besp/dryer-vent-seal.html

[2] Kill-A-Watt: http://www.energyefficientchoices.com/products/kill-a-watt-meter.html

[3] Energy Saving Smart Strip: http://www.energyefficientchoices.com/products/energy-saving-smart-strip.html

Chapter 2

[1] Trane: http://www.trane.com

Ingersoll-Rand Company
Corporate Center
155 Chestnut Ridge Road
Montvale, NJ 07645

Telephone: 201-573-0123

[2] solar powered exhaust vent: http://www.energyefficientchoices.com/products/besp/solar-powered-exhaust-vent.html

Chapter 3

[1] E-Teck residential high-efficiency heat pump water heaters: http://www.aers.com/etech_residential_water_heating.html

Applied Energy Recovery Systems, Inc.
6670A Corners Industrial Court
Norcross, GA 30092

Phone: (770) 734-9696
Fax: (770) 453-9323

2 Tankless Electric Water Heaters: http://www.energyefficientchoices.com/
products/stiebel-tankless-electric-water-heater.html

3 Solar Estimate: http://www.energyefficientchoices.com/resources/solar-
power-sizing-calculator.html

4 Moen: http://www.moen.com

Moen Incorporated
25300 Al Moen Drive
North Olmsted, OH 44070

Tel: (440) 962-2000

Chapter 4

1 Nanosolar: http://www.nanosolar.com

Nanosolar, Inc.
5521 Hellyer Avenue
San Jose, CA 95138

Fax: 408.365.5965

2 Solar Power Sizing Calculator: http://www.energyefficientchoices.com/
resources/solar-power-sizing-calculator.html

3 Wind Energy Sizing Calculator: http://www.energyefficientchoices.com/
resources/wind-power-system-sizing-calculator.html

4 Skystream 3.7 by Southwest Windpower: http://www.skystreamenergy.
   com and http://www.energyefficientchoices.com/products/skystream-
   wind-generator.html

>   Southwest Windpower
>   1801 W. Route 6
>   Flagstaff, AZ 86001
>
>   Phone: 928-779-9463

5 Net Metering Policies + Green Power Markets: http://www.eere.energy.
   gov/greenpower/markets/netmetering.shtml

Chapter 5

1 Phoenix Electric SUV: http://www.phoenixmotorcars.com/

>   Phoenix MC
>   401 S. Doubleday Avenue
>   Ontario, CA 91761
>
>   Phone: +1.909.987.0815

2 Alternative Fuel Finder: http://www.eere.energy.gov/afdc/stations/find_
   station.php

3 Natural Gas Refilling Stations: http://www.eere.energy.gov/afdc/fuels/
   natural_gas_locations.html

4 Pickens Plan: http://www.energyefficientchoices.com/pickens-plan/

Chapter 6

1 HUD Web site: http://www.hud.gov

U.S. Department of Housing and Urban
Development
451 Seventh Street S.W.
Washington, DC 20410

Telephone: (202) 708-1112
TTY: (202) 708-1455

[2] VA Web site: http://www.va.gov/

Department of Veterans Affairs
810 Vermont Avenue NW
Washington, DC 20420

[3] Fannie Mae Web site: http://www.fanniemae.com/

Corporate Headquarters
3900 Wisconsin Avenue, NW
Washington, DC 20016-2892

Phone: (202) 752-7000

[4] DSIRE (Database of State Incentives for Renewables and Efficiency):
http://www.dsireusa.org/

Chapter 7

[1] Solar Power Sizing Calculator: http://www.energyefficientchoices.com/
resources/solar-power-sizing-calculator.html

[2] Wind Energy Sizing Calculator: http://www.energyefficientchoices.com/
resources/wind-power-system-sizing-calculator.html

[3] Net Metering Policies: http://www.eere.energy.gov/greenpower/markets/
netmetering.shtml

Appendix A

Common R-Values

Insulating Material	R Value per Inch	R Value Total Thickness
Insulation Materials		
Fiberglass Batt	3.14-4.30	
Fiberglass Blown (attic)	2.20-4.30	
Fiberglass Blown (wall)	3.70-4.30	
Rock Wool Batt	3.14-4.00	
Rock Wool Blown (attic)	3.10-4.00	
Rock Wool Blown (wall)	3.10-4.00	
Cellulose Blown (attic)	3.13	
Cellulose Blown (wall)	3.7	
Vermiculite	2.13	
Autoclaved Aerated Concrete	1.05	
Urea Terpolymer Foam	4.48	
Rigid Fiberglass (> 4lb/ft3)	4	
Expanded Polystyrene (beadboard)	4	
Extruded Polystyrene	5	
Polyurethane (foamed-in-place)	6.25	
Polyisocyanurate (foil-faced)	7.2	
Construction Materials		
Concrete Block 4"		0.8
Concrete Block 8"		1.11
Concrete Block 12"		1.28
Brick 4" common		0.8
Brick 4" face		0.44
Poured Concrete	0.08	
Softwood Lumber	1.25	
2" nominal (1 1/2")		1.88
2x4 (3 1/2")		4.38
2x6 (5 1/2")		6.88
Cedar Logs and Lumber	1.33	
Sheathing Materials		
Plywood	1.25	
1/4"		0.31

3/8"		0.47
1/2"		0.63
5/8"		0.77
3/4"		0.94
Fiberboard	2.64	
1/2"		1.32
25/32"		2.06
Fiberglass (3/4")		3
(1")		4
(1 1/2")		6
Extruded Polystyrene (3/4")		3.75
(1")		5
(1 1/2")		7.5
Foil-faced Polyisocyanurate (3/4")		5.4
(1")		7.2
(1 1/2")		10.8
Plywood (5/8")		0.77
(3/4")		0.93
Wood Bevel Lapped		0.8
Aluminum, Steel, Vinyl (hollow backed)		0.61
(w/ 1/2" Insulating board)		1.8
Brick 4"		0.44
Interior Finish Materials		
Gypsum Board (drywall 1/2")		0.45
(5/8")		0.56
Paneling (3/8")		0.47
Flooring Materials		
Plywood	1.25	
(3/4")		0.93
Particle Board (underlay)	1.31	
(5/8")		0.82
Hardwood Flooring	0.91	
(3/4")		0.68
Tile, Linoleum		0.05
Carpet (fibrous pad)		2.08
(rubber pad)		1.23
Roofing Materials		
Asphalt Shingles		0.44
Wood Shingles		0.97

Windows		
Single Glass		0.91
w/storm		2
Double-insulating glass (3/16") air space		1.61
(1/4" air space)		1.69
(1/2" air space)		2.04
(3/4" air space)		2.38
(1/2" w/ Low-E 0.20)		3.13
(w/ suspended film)		2.77
(w/ 2 suspended films)		3.85
(w/ suspended film and low-E)		4.05
Triple-insulating glass (1/4" air spaces)		2.56
(1/2" air spaces)		3.23
Addition for tight-fitting drapes or shades, or closed blinds		0.29
Doors		
Wood Hollow Core Flush (1 3/4")		2.17
Solid Core Flush (1 3/4")		3.03
Solid Core Flush (2 1/4")		3.7
Panel Door w/ 7/16" Panels (1 3/4")		1.85
Storm Door (wood 50% glass)		1.25
(metal)		1
Metal Insulating (2" w/ urethane)		15
Air Films		
Interior Ceiling		0.61
Interior Wall		0.68
Exterior		0.17
Air Spaces		
1/2" to 4" approximately		1

Index

i denotes an illustration, picture, or photo; *t* denotes a table; *fig* denotes a figure

U

uninterruptible power supply (UPS),
16, 90
unplugging appliances, advantages of,
15
UPS (uninterruptible power supply),
16, 90
U.S. Department of Energy, 53, 62, 75
U.S. Department of Housing and
Urban Development (HUD), 94
U.S. Environmental Protection Agency,
61
U.S.-supplied fuels, 78
utility companies, 53, 56, 60, 75
utility cost savings, 69

V

VA (Department of Veterans Affairs),
and energy-efficient based mortgages,
66, 94
VAWT (vertical axis wind turbine),
52–53, 74, 90
vegetables, canned vs. frozen, 19
vehicle power, options for, 57. *See also
specific types*
vehicles. *See also specific types*
consumer preferences for, 57–58
operating costs of, 58–59
technological innovations in, 57
types of, 58–63
vents, 7, 8. *See also* cooking vents; ridge
vents; solar powered exhaust vents
vertical axis wind turbine (VAWT),
52–53, 74, 90
voltage, 54, 81, 83

W

washing machines, 12–13, 42, 72
water, for drinking, 19
water heating systems, 7, 22, 35–42,
72–73
water purifier, 19
water usage, hot, 1, 35, 40–42
watts

defined, 90
wasted, cost for, 14*fig*
weather, protection from, 32
weather conditions, and solar
efficiencies, 48–49. *See also* climate
entries
Web sites
alternative fuel finder, 64, 93
Department of Veterans Affairs (VA),
66, 70, 94
dryer vent seal, 20, 91
DSIRE (Database of State Incentives
for Renewables and Efficiency),
70, 94
energy saving smart strip, 20, 91
E-Teck residential high-efficiency
heat pump water heaters, 43, 91
Fannie Mae, 66, 70, 94
Findsolar.com, 48
HUD, 70, 93
Kill-A-Watt meter, 20, 91
Moen (company), 43, 92
Nanosolar (company), 56, 64, 92
natural gas refilling stations, 93
net metering policies, 56, 78, 93, 94
Phoenix Electric SUV, 63, 93
Pickens Plan, 64, 93
Skystream 3.7 by Southwest
Windpower, 43, 56, 93
solar estimate, 92
solar power sizing calculator, 56, 78,
92, 94
solar powered exhaust vents, 33, 91
tankless electric water heaters, 43, 92
Trane (company), 33, 91
U.S. Department of Energy, 53
VA (Department of Veterans Affairs),
66, 70, 94
wind energy sizing calculator, 56, 78,
92, 94
wind energy sizing calculator, 51, 56,
74, 78, 92, 94
wind farms, 23
wind turbine power/systems
advantages of, 51

Printed in the United States
by Baker & Taylor Publisher Services